Hiking in the Grand Canyon Backcountry

A no nonsense guide to Grand Canyon

J. D. GREEN

editing and technical advice

JIM OHLMAN

TOWER OF RA PUBLISHING

Tower of Ra Publishing
John D. Green
Editor: Jim Ohlman
Hiking in the Grand Canyon Backcountry
A no nonsense guide to Grand Canyon
First Edition, Second Printing

International Standard Book Number
Hardback 0-9644893-1-7;
Paperback 0-9644893-0-9;

Library of Congress Card Catalog Number: 95-60196

Tower of Ra Publishing, 1501 Tina Lane, Kissimmee, FL 34744
Printed in the United States by Rose Printing Company, Inc., Tallahassee, Florida
Typesetting by Suzi Harris

Mount Sinyala on the Esplanade below Great Thumb Mesa.
Photo By: Bob Marley

Eastern Grand Canyon
Photo By: G. Henshaw

Bright Angel Trail below Indian Garden
Photo By: G. Henshaw

TABLE OF CONTENTS

Colorado River at the foot of the Whitmore Trail.

Granite Gorge of Colorado River as viewed from Clear Creek Trail; Dec. 22, 1935.
NPS Photo   Grand Canyon National Park #470

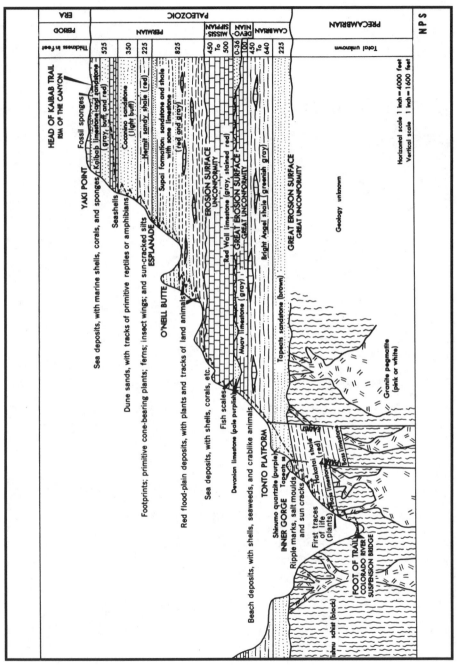

Geologic Cross Section.

National Park Service

Introduction

Hiking Grand Canyon can be a very enjoyable experience. Yet every year many hikers die and still more are rescued from the great chasm. Dangers from heat, lack of water, loose rock, snakes and during the colder months, hypothermia, are immense. The last thing the author would want is someone to die in the Canyon with this guidebook in their rucksack!

There are some precautions to be taken before entering into Grand Canyon and the National Park Service has a Backcountry Office that will help line people out for hikes. In the heavily used areas, such as "The Main Corridor" reservations may have to be made in advance. The Park Service can also inform you on current trail conditions. Be wise and talk with the Rangers first.

Clothing should be light weight and loose especially during the warmer months and wool can be pleasant during the cold months. A hat is essential for shielding the hiker from the sun, and helps prevent hypothermia during the winter.

Boots are a good idea in rough terrain. Many people wear tennis shoes on the Main Corridor trails. Regardless of the type shoe it is essential that they fit well and are comfortable. Shoes that are new, or inadequately broke in have a tendency to blister the hiker's feet. Very heavy mountaineering boots intended for Alaska or Colorado are not designed for use in the Grand Canyon environment. Some people prefer light weight construction boots, or old military boots. Snakes in the backcountry, along with brush, cactus and sharp rock present serious problems outside the maintained trails of the Main Corridor. I cannot emphasize enough the importance of comfortable, yet durable light weight foot wear.

For just about all trips into the Canyon a backpack is necessary to carry food, sleeping bag, poncho and lots of water. It should be large enough to carry the gear for the length of the outing whether it is a day hike to Plateau Point or a week long outing on the Tuckup Trail.

A walking stick is an interesting option and the author has used one when carrying heavy loads in the more remote portions of Grand Canyon.

This guide was designed to be an outline for most of the major canyons in the Grand. Topographical maps on a usable scale are a must and may be

I

purchased either in the Park, at various backpacking stores, or through the U.S.G.S.

Water sources in the remote reaches are not always reliable and depending upon drought, there can be a great variance from year to year in springs and pothole water.

Also, do not carry on your back more than one-third of your body weight when hiking. Not only is it bad for the body's frame, but carrying out 70 pounds of gear while gaining 5,000 feet of elevation is energy inefficient.

Be safe, be efficient, be happy!

Pictographs along the top of Bright Angel Trail; some estimate these drawings to be 800 years old.
Photo By: Berezenko, NPS   Grand Canyon National Park #10,993

II

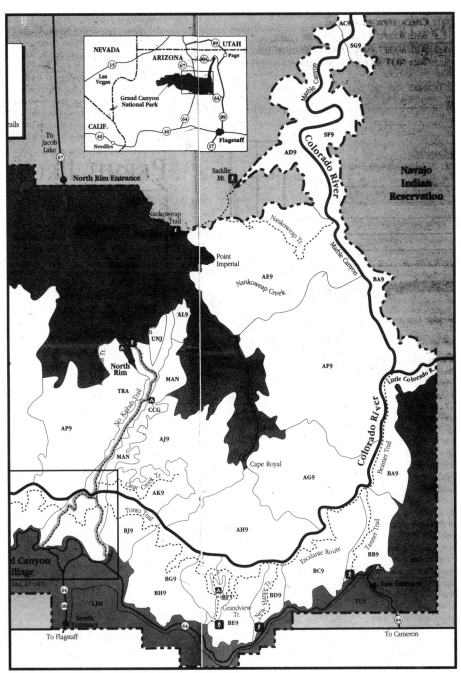

Backcountry Use Areas.   Courtesy of NPS Grand Canyon National Park

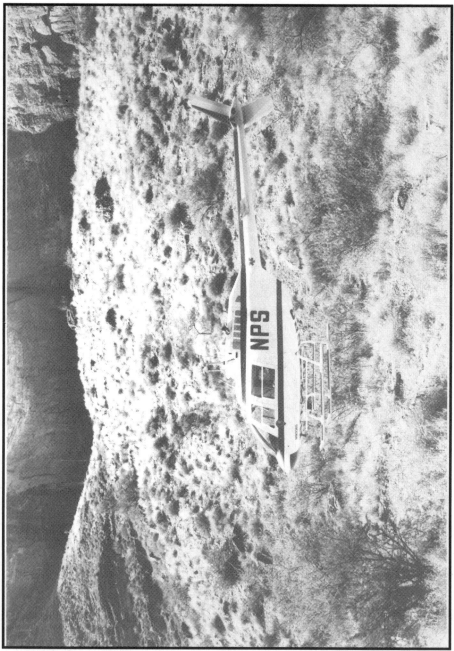

Medivac helicopter landing at Indian Garden.
1985 NPS   Grand Canyon National Park #11,780

Rules and Regulations

Grand Canyon National Park Backcountry use Regulations

The 1916 National Park Service Organic Act and the 1978 Public Law 95-250 require the National Park Service "to conserve" park resources, and the values and purposes for which the park was established as well as "to provide for the enjoyment" of those resources and values "in such a manner and by such means as will leave them unimpaired for the enjoyment of future generations." Conscientious care is necessary to preserve and protect natural and cultural resources while still providing opportunities for public enjoyment of backcountry lands.

Backcountry use regulations are based on the Grand Canyon National Park Backcountry Management Plan, Title 36 Code of Federal Regulations (for Parks, Forests, and Public Property), and related federal legislation. Your cooperation is needed to help preserve and protect the Natural and Cultural resources. It is your responsibility to know and obey the following regulations while in the backcountry. Failure to obey backcountry regulations may result in a fine or appearance before a United States Magistrate.

1. A Backcountry Use Permit *is required for all overnight Backcountry use* and **MUST** be in your possession while in the Backcountry. 36 CFR 1.6
2. Wood or charcoal fires are prohibited. However, the use of sterno or backpack stove is permitted. 36 CFR 2.13
3. Carry out your trash. Burning or burying of trash or toilet paper is prohibited. 36 CFR 2.14
4. Firearms, bows and arrows are prohibited. 36 CFR 2.4
5. Pets must be restrained at all times. Pets are prohibited below the rim. 36 CFR 2.15
6. Leaving a trail or walkway to shortcut between portions of the same trail or walkway, or to shortcut to an adjacent trail or walkway is

V

prohibited. 36 CFR 2.1

7. Tossing, throwing or rolling rocks or other items inside caves or caverns, into valleys, canyons, or caverns, down hillsides or mountain sides or into thermal features is prohibited. 36 CFR 2.1

8. The feeding, touching, teasing, frightening or intentional disturbing of wildlife nesting breeding or other activities is prohibited. 36 CFR 2.2

9. Possessing, destroying, injuring, defacing, removing, digging, or disturbing from its natural state any plants, rocks, animals, minerals, cultural or archeological resources are prohibited. 36 CFR 2.1

10. The use of motorized vehicles or wheeled vehicles, such as motorcycles, buggies, bicycles, and similar vehicles, on trails above or below the rim is prohibited. 36 CFR 4.2, 4.10 and 4.30

11. Fishing by persons 14 years or older requires a valid Arizona fishing license or nonresident permit. 36 CFR 2.3

12. Writing, scratching, or otherwise defacing property signs, buildings, or other objects is prohibited. 36 CFR 2.31

13. Private stock use requires a Backcountry Use Permit and must comply with the Grand Canyon National Park Private Stock Use Policies, as found in Appendix D, of the Backcountry Management Plan. 36 CFR 2.16

14. Only one group from an organization may camp in a designated campground or non-Corridor Use Area per night.

15. The use of soap in creeks or camping within 100 feet of any water source is prohibited. 36 CFR 2.10

16. The Backcountry Use Permit is valid only for the itinerary and dates specified on the permit. 36 CFR 1.6

17. Commercial Use of the backcountry must be authorized by concession permit or commercial use license. 36 CFR 5.3

18. Violating a closure, designation, use or activity restriction or condition, schedule of visiting hours, or public use limit is prohibited. 36 CFR 1.5

Backcountry Reservation and Permit System

Reservations and Permits

The Backcountry Use Permit is currently free and is required for *all overnight use* of the backcountry except in the dormitories or cabins at Phantom Ranch. The Backcountry Use Permit is valid only for the itinerary and dates specified. Backcountry travelers must have their permit in their possession while in the backcountry. Once a camp is established, the permit must be attached to pack, tent, or other equipment in plain view to be easily checked by rangers. Permits are not required for day hiking or day riding. However, day users must observe all other backcountry use regulations.

Permits may often be obtained the day a backcountry trip is to begin, but advance reservations are recommended. The demand for permits during the spring and fall months, on holidays, and during the summer vacation period far exceeds the use limits that have been established to protect the resource and the quality of the user's backpacking experience. If reservations are made, the Backcountry Use Permit must be picked up *in person* no later than *9:00 a.m. Mountain Standard Time* on the day the trip begins. WHEN A PERMIT IS NOT CLAIMED BY THIS DEADLINE, THE ENTIRE TRIP IS AUTOMATICALLY CANCELLED. Permits can be claimed throughout the year at the South Rim Backcountry Reservations Office and, during the summer session, at the North Rim Backcountry Reservations Office (mid-May through late October).

Reservations and/or permits may sometimes be obtained from rangers on duty at the Tuweep, Meadview, and Lees Ferry Ranger Stations. However, these rangers have other patrol responsibilities and may not be available to provide assistance. Consequently, it is recommended that trips be planned in advance through the Backcountry Reservations Office to be certain of permit availability. Also, the National Park Service is working with Bureau of Land Management offices in St. George and Kanab, Utah, to arrange for these offices to issue permits for a limited number of Use Areas.

Reservation requests for overnight backcountry use are accepted by mail or in person only. Reservation requests for overnight backcountry use are accepted by mail or in person only. Beginning with the first day of a month, permit requests will be accepted for a proposed trip starting on any date in that month or the following four (4) months. For example, beginning on December 1, 1996, permit requests for any start date through April 30th, 1997 would be accepted.

Backcountry Reservations Office
P.O. Box 129
Grand Canyon, AZ 86023

For recorded information about taking a trip into the Grand Canyon Backcountry call: (520) 638-7888.

Makeshift log ladder in Jumpup Canyon.

Code	Use Area Name	Management Zone	Camping Type	Code	Use Area Name	Management Zone	Camping Type
AA9	Badger	Primitive	A/L	BR9	Garnet	Primitive	A/L
AB9	Rider	Primitive	A/L	BSN	The Basin	Threshold	Day Use
AC9	South Canyon	Primitive	A/L	BS9	Fossil	Wild	A/L
AD9	Saddle Canyon	Primitive	A/L	BT9	Olo	Wild	A/L
AE9	Nankoweap	Primitive	A/L	BU9	National	Wild	A/L
AF9	Chuar	Wild	A/L		Corridor		
AG9	Unkar	Wild	A/L	CBG	– Bright Angel	Corridor	D/G
AH9	Vishnu	Wild	A/L	CCG	– Cottonwood	Corridor	D/G
AJ9	Cheyava	Wild	A/L	CIG	– Indian Garden	Corridor	D/G
AK9	Clear Creek	Threshold	A/L	LA9	Kanab Creek	Primitive	A/L
AL9	Greenland Springs	Wild	A/L	LB9	Boysag	Wild	A/L
AM9	Surprise Valley	Primitive	A/L	LC9	The Dome	Primitive	A/L
AP9	Phantom Creek	Wild	A/L	LE9	Parashant	Wild	A/L
AQ9	Trinity Creek	Wild	A/L	LF9	Trail Canyon	Wild	A/L
AR9	Scorpion Ridge	Wild	A/L	LG9	Diamond Creek	Wild	A/L
AS9	North Bass	Primitive	A/L	LH9	Separation	Wild	A/L
AT9	Powell Plateau	Primitive	A/L	LI9	Whitmore	Threshold	A/L
AU9	Blacktail Canyon	Wild	A/L	LJM	Long Jim	Threshold	A/L
AV9	Tapeats Amphitheater	Wild	A/L	LJ9	Surprise	Wild	A/L
	Tapeats			LK9	Burnt Point	Wild	A/L
AW7	– Upper Tapeats	Threshold	D/S	LL9	Snap Point	Primitive	A/L
AW8	– Lower Tapeats	Threshold	D/S	LM9	Grand Wash Cliffs	Primitive	A/L
AX9	Deer Creek	Primitive	A/L	MAN	Manzanita	Threshold	Day Use
AY9	Esplanade	Primitive	A/L	NA9	Walhalla Plateau	Primitive	A/L
AZ9	Fishtail	Wild	A/L	NB9	Thompson Canyon	Primitive	A/L
BA9	Palisades	Primitive	A/L	ND9	Robbers Roost	Primitive	A/L
BB9	Tanner	Primitive	A/L	NF9	Widforss	Threshold	A/L
BC9	Cardenas	Primitive	A/L	NG9	Outlet	Primitive	A/L
BD9	Red Canyon	Primitive	A/L	NH9	Point Sublime	Threshold	A/L
BE9	Hance Creek	Primitive	A/L	NJ9	Swamp Ridge	Primitive	A/L
BF5	Horseshoe Mesa	Threshold	D/S	NK9	Kanab Point	Primitive	A/L
BG9	Cottonwood Creek	Primitive	A/L	NL9	Tuckup Point	Primitive	A/L
BH9	Grapevine	Primitive	A/L	NM9	Toroweap Valley	Threshold	A/L
BJ9	Cremation	Primitive	A/L	NN9	Lava	Threshold	A/L
	Monument			SA9	Cape Solitude	Primitive	A/L
BL4	– Horn Creek	Threshold	D/S	SB9	Cedar Mountain	Threshold	A/L
BL5	– Salt Creek	Threshold	D/S	SE9	Pasture Wash	Threshold	A/L
BL6	– Cedar Spring	Threshold	D/S	SF9	Eminence Break	Primitive	A/L
BL7	– Monument Creek	Threshold	D/S	SG9	Shinumo Wash	Primitive	A/L
BL8	– Granite Rapids	Threshold	D/S	SH9	Saltwater Wash	Primitive	A/L
	Hermit			SI9	Jackass	Primitive	A/L
BM7	– Hermit Creek	Threshold	D/S	TRA	Transept	Threshold	Day Use
BM8	– Hermit Rapids	Threshold	D/S	TUS	Tusayan	Threshold	Day Use
BN9	Boucher	Primitive	A/L	UNJ	Uncle Jim Point	Threshold	Day Use
BO9	Slate	Primitive	A/L	A/L	= At-Large Camping		
BP9	Ruby	Primitive	A/L	D/G	= Designated Campground		
BQ9	South Bass	Primitive	A/L	D/S	= Designated Site Camping		

Corridor Zone Recommended for hikers without previous experience at the Grand Canyon. Maintained trails. Purified water stations. Paved roads to trailheads. Toilets, signs, emergency phones, and ranger stations. Use of private livestock (horses and mules only) allowed only with permit.

Threshold Zone Recommended for experienced canyon hikers. Non-maintained trails. Scarce water sources. Dirt roads to trailheads. Pit toilets. Use of private livestock (horses and mules only) allowed with permit only on Whitmore Trail and on designated roads and trails on the rim.

Primitive Zone Recommended for highly experienced canyon hikers with proven route-finding ability. Non-maintained trails and routes. 4-wheel-drive roads to trailheads. Occasional signs. No other developments. Use of private livestock (horses and mules only) allowed with permit only on the Ken Patrick Trail to Uncle Jim Trail to Uncle Jim Point, and on designated roads on the rim.

Wild Zone Recommended for highly experienced canyon hikers with extensive route-finding ability. Indistinct to non-existent routes require advanced route-finding ability. Water sources scarce to non-existent. No other development. Use of private livestock is not allowed.

Primitive and Wild Zones are not recommended for use during summer months due to extreme high temperatures and the lack of reliable water sources.

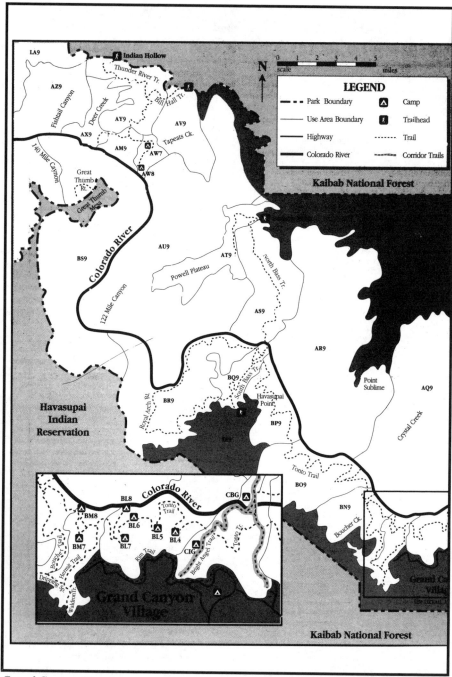

Grand Canyon Use Areas.   Courtesy of National Park Service, Grand Canyon

Park Service Reservations must be made through the Backcountry Reservations Office, but permits can be picked up at Lee's Ferry, Lake Mead, Tuweep and Pipe Springs.

For areas outside the National Park, hikers may contact:

Havasupai Tribal Enterprises
Supai, AZ 86435
(520) 448-2121

Hualapai Wildlife and Outdoor Recreational Department
P.O. Box 216
Peach Springs, AZ 86434
(520) 769-2227

Parks and Recreation Department
Navajo Nation
P.O. Box 308
Window Rock, AZ 86515
(520) 871-6647

Bureau of Land Management
Arizona Strip District
390 N. 350 E.
St. George, UT 84770
(801) 673-3545

Another interesting contact more literary in nature:

Grand Canyon Association
P.O. Box 399
Grand Canyon, AZ 86023
(520) 638-2481

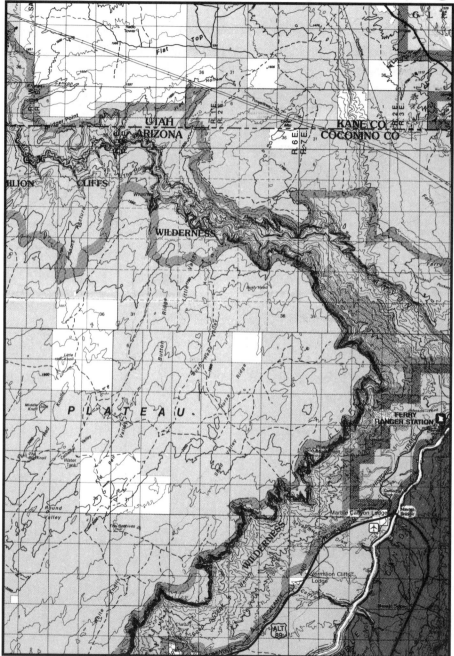

Map of Paria River Canyon; Paria is a Paiute word meaning muddy water.
Courtesy of Arizona Strip District Bureau of Land Management

Marble Canyon

Lee's Ferry

River rafters start their journey down the Colorado River through Grand Canyon at Lee's Ferry and during the warmer months you will see them rigging their rafts daily at the public launch located here. Fishermen like this area too, as trout fishing in the cold water below Glen Canyon Dam has produced many trophy size fish. There are many hiking opportunities around Lee's Ferry, along with a few overnighter possibilities as well.

John D. Lee established a ferry here in 1871 for the Mormon Church. He built a ranch house at Lonely Dell which is still standing today. On the Shinarump Bench above Lee's Ferry stands Johnson Point, named after Warren M. Johnson who took charge of the Ferry after J. D. Lee's arrest. Lee was accused and convicted of taking part in the Mountain Meadows massacre and executed in 1877.[1]

All distance along the Colorado River is gauged in miles upstream or downstream of Lee's Ferry, which is taken to be mile 0. Thus, Navajo Bridge is located at river mile 4.5 and Glen Canyon Dam at River Mile -16. Additionally, direction along the river is referenced to a person looking downstream. Jackass Canyon is on river left (or left bank) while Badger Creek is on river right, and Cathedral Wash is upstream of Navajo Bridge while being downstream of the Paria River confluence.

It is possible to walk the left bank upstream from Lee's Ferry, but hikers are stopped short of Glen Canyon Dam. In his book "The Romance of the Colorado River" Frederick Dellenbaugh made an interesting note about the river; "I remember once hearing that a great many years ago it was frozen over in the neighborhood of Lee's Ferry, where for a little distance the current is not rapid." Rumor has it that after raiding sheep from a Mormon rancher in southern Utah, a band of Navajos crossed the frozen river at Lee's Ferry and herded their ill-gotten charges into Hislop Cave, a large alcove on river left at mile - 3.0.[2]

Since the construction of Glen Canyon Dam in the early 1960's, water temperatures at Lee's Ferry are constant and flow fluctuations moderate. Winter freeze up is highly unlikely. It's presence has also greatly reduced silt flow down the Colorado; most of which now is trapped behind the dam in Lake Powell. Many hikers and nature lovers regret the loss of Glen Canyon beneath the waters of Lake Powell, as it was one of the most splendid canyons along the Colorado River.

On the Echo Cliffs above the Lonely Dell is the Spencer Trail, which is said to have been laid out part by man and part by mule. Charlie Spencer had a gold mining operation here at the Ferry, and 1/2 mile upstream of the Ferry on river right are the submerged remains of a steamship. He hauled coal from Glen Canyon down to his mining operation. The boiler may still be seen on the slope above the river.[3]

Up Paria River, on the northeast side of that canyon, the Escalante-Dominguez Trail makes a way up through the Echo Cliffs. In 1776, Escalante, Dominguez and their entourage crossed the Arizona Strip, but failed to find a ford on the Colorado River. The expedition reached the river in the area of Marble Canyon in two places, but they were unable to locate a crossing. Rations were so low that they killed and ate some of their horses. They eventually located a crossing farther up in what is now Lake Powell.[4]

Paria River Canyon has a famous narrows section that hikers enjoy, but flash floods can be deadly. An alternate route down from Utah, also prone to flooding is the Buckskin Gulch which joins the Paria. It requires wading through stagnant pools and a rope may be necessary at one point for non-climbers. Hikers have climbed far up into a nameless canyon to the northwest of the Lonely Dell.

Downriver travel below Lee's Ferry on river right is possible, but hikers must negotiate a short cliff immediately downstream of Cathedral Wash. It is possible to climb out to the highway via Cathedral Wash, Soap Creek and Rider Canyon, but not via Badger Creek. Other, less advertised routes exist between Navajo Bridge and Badger Creek and a good fisherman route can be found at Mile 8.5

Across the Colorado River opposite Lee's Ferry, the Buzzard Highline trail climbs to the top of the Echo Peaks by way of the obvious sand slide. An alternate way to reach the peaks starts near the Marble Canyon Bridge and is known as the Echo Peaks Trail (or C. C. C. Trail). On their lower ends these two trails are connected by the Dugway Road, which was once part of the old Ferry road leading in from the south. Upper Dugway is more scenic, but not as useful for the hiker; while Lower Dugway is great for fishermen and is the easiest route along the left bank between Lee's Ferry and the Echo Peaks/ CCC Trail. This road became known as the "Honeymoon Trail," as couples would make the trek from Arizona to St. George, Utah to marry in the Temple there.[5]

Cathedral Wash

It is less than two miles down Cathedral Wash to the Colorado River from the Lee's Ferry road. Several falls must be bypassed and they make the route hard enough to be interesting. Although small when compared to most of the canyons in the Grand, Cathedral is an impressive little canyon. Much of the hike is through red shale and sandstone of the Triassic Moenkopi formation. Cathedral Wash is a good day hike for a first time visitor to the Lee's Ferry area.[6]

Hikers may walk upstream from Cathedral Wash along the river to Lee's Ferry. Downstream travel is hindered by a cliff at about Mile 3.2, but it can be negotiated with some hand and toe climbing. Near the bridge a ramp rises above the river and hikers must follow this ledge on their way to Soap Creek. A ravine near Mile 6 allows hikers to scramble back down to the river and continue on to Soap.

Fifteen hundred feet above Cathedral Wash, across the Lee's Ferry Road, is Lowery Spring where a good flow of water can always be found. Hikers should park their car at the pullout due south of where Lee's Ferry Road crosses Cathedral Wash.

There are no confirmed trails or routes through the Vermillion Cliffs to the Paria Plateau between Paria Canyon and Jacob's Pools (Sand Crack), but a long standing rumor has it that a sheep trail reaches the plateau rim, somewhere behind the Lowery Spring.[7]

C C C Trail

Navajo sheep herders use this trail to access the river via the wash at about Mile 3.8. This is an extension of the Echo Peaks Trail and there are signs of construction at places along the route. There is a nice beach at the river, but travel both up and down river is difficult; although some bold hikers have made it down river to Jackass Canyon. This route is used extensively by fishermen.[8]

Jackass Canyon

Jackass Canyon has a route from the rim to the river, but it does contain a tricky section near the river. A fixed rope is necessary in one place where a 20 foot fall crosses the drainage. The ring bolt anchor at the fall in Jackass Canyon was removed some time prior to 11/11/94, so any party using this route should have at least one competent climber/scrambler along.

John Annerino states in his guide that pirate river runners have been caught by the National Park Service trying to put their boats in the river via this canyon.[9]

This three mile round trip makes a good introductory hike for Marble Canyon. It is possible to continue downstream from the mouth of Jackass Canyon, but upstream travel is barred by difficult to pass cliffs beneath Navajo Bridge. It is nearly 8 miles from Lee's Ferry to Jackass Canyon via the river. Overland access is via a dirt road heading west from the ADOT yard at Navajo Spring. Follow the road 1 1/2 miles to a well used parking area.

All hiking on the Navajo Indian Reservation requires a permit available through the mail. Overnight camping anywhere within GCNP requires a separate permit available at Lee's Ferry River Ranger Station or through South Rim Backcountry Reservations Office.

Badger Canyon

Several cliffs bar progress for a ropeless rim to river route in this canyon, although climbers have completed a route by making three rappels. A 100 foot rope is needed if you plan on pulling your rope down behind you and come out a different route such as Soap Creek or Cathedral Wash. At the river the main attraction is Badger Rapid.

Fisherman's Route

A route at mile 8.5 (right bank) is used extensively by fishermen. Ask locally for directions. Ledges in the Kaibab limestone and two airy ledges in the Toroweap make this route less than safe for small children.

Soap Creek

Soap Creek has a route from the rim to the river. The north fork is blocked by a high fall but the south fork goes and will take hikers to the river. This canyon is most easily accessed via a ravine near the south end of the airstrip near Cliff Dwellers Lodge.[10]

Salt Water Wash

It is about four miles from the rim to the river down Salt Water Wash. A good loop trip is down Salt Water and out Tanner Wash. When going downstream it is necessary to stay on a rising bench of Supai rimrock in order to reach Tanner Wash. Hikers can also boulder hop up river to Jackass Canyon from here. A parking area due west of Red Point along the highway provides access for this wash. Watch for steep sections through the Coconino sandstone.[11]

Tanner Wash

Hikers can go down Tanner Wash to the Supai rim and a route to the river is achieved by heading upstream towards Salt Water Wash. Much nearer the mouth of Tanner, Butchart and others have encountered problems finding a route to the river.[12] A good loop hike is down Tanner and out Salt Water Wash. Problems in this wash include bypassing a huge pouroff to the west and then carefully descending a steep talus back into the wash bed. Access is via the main wash from Tanner Well, or closer, by a cross country route west of the Highway 89/89A junction.

5

Hot Na Na

The bed of Hot Na Na goes to the Supai redrock with just one rough section in the Coconino. Hikers may reach the river by contouring downriver atop the Supai to a ravine at Mile 18.5. A good loop trip is down Tanner along the Supai rimrock and out Hot Na Na. Jim Ohlman and I were able to go down the bed of Hot Na Na, head downriver along the ledges and climb out Shinumo Wash all on one long weekend. Access for this canyon is the same as for Tanner Wash (via Tanner Well).[13]

Rider Canyon

There is a rim to river route in Rider Canyon and it is easiest to start off its south rim, west of the neck (or narrowest part) of Rider Point.[14] A large section of cliff has separated itself form the rest of the rim and this seems to be the easiest place to get down to the bed. The map shows a spring in upper Rider and going to the river is not too difficult. One can also stay on the Supai rim and hike upstream to an exit out Soap Creek. It is also possible to walk a ways downriver from Rider along the river bank. A large boulder, the size of a house, constricts the flow of the Colorado River and thus the name Boulder Narrows. There is no direct river route between Rider and North.

There is a route to the rim at about river mile 19. Here a ravine provides access to the Supai rim rock and some route finding in the Coconino and Kaibab will allow one to reach the rim. From river mile 19 it is possible to contour along the top of the Supai into North Canyon where hikers may reach the rim. Access to the Colorado River from the top of the Supai is more than a mile beyond North Canyon. One can also follow a route which starts along the river at Mile 19, and then ascends several Supai cliffs before reaching North Canyon. This variation will allow direct access into lower North Canyon and then down to the river at it's mouth.

Aitchinson (1985) has a good road log for getting to the Rider Canyon route, and a good route description as well.[15]

North Canyon

No ropeless, rim to river route exists in North Canyon to my knowledge. It is possible to hike down from the head of North

6

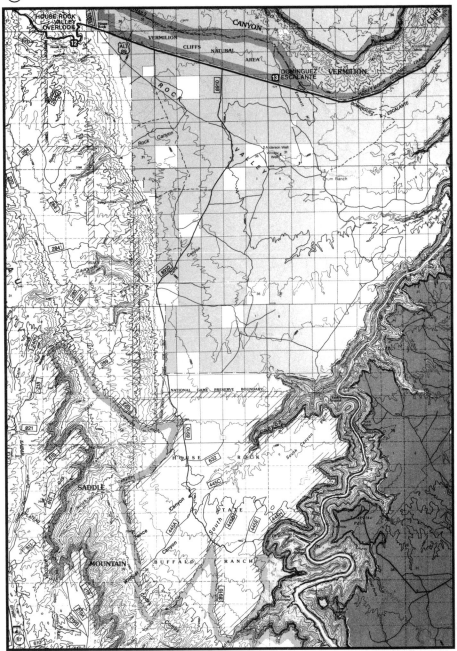

Topo Map of Marble Canyon.

Courtesy of Arizona Strip District Bureau of Land Management.

7

Second Powell Expedition. Water polished Redwall limestone appeared to be like Marble; J.W. Powell dubbed this section of the Grand, "Marble Canyon."
Photo By: Jack Hillers 1872   Grand Canyon National Park #17,249

8

Canyon, but there are barrier falls in the Supai drainage. One and one half miles down river from North Canyon hikers can descend the Supai to the Colorado via a very steep ravine, or one can continue another 3/4 mile to an easier and safer route. Upriver access to the Colorado is via the ravine near Mile 19.

Farther up on the Kaibab Plateau, above House Rock Valley, the North Canyon Trail leads down to the Cocks Comb. The easiest access to this trail is north of the National Park boundary via a road that leaves the pavement one mile south of Kaibab Lodge. This Forest Service Road #610 has forks to Saddle Mountain, Dog Point and East Rim Viewpoints. The North Canyon Trail can be reached by following the signs out to East Rim. North Canyon Trail is a relatively short day hike of about 10 miles round trip. North Canyon and Crystal Springs are reliable sources of water. Beyond the Cocks Comb the Arizona Game and Fish Department established a buffalo ranch and maintains a herd of about 100 animals.[16]

Shinumo Wash

During a traverse on top of the Redwall from Hot Na Na to Shinumo Wash, Jim Ohlman and I stopped in Tiger Wash for water. There is a deep plunge pool here that should be reliable. The bowl like rim of the pool was steep enough to make us use a rope to fill canteens. I helped Jim down with the rope and he filled the canteens and sent them up to me. I had to hold the rope tightly and brace my feet against a large boulder so Jim could climb back up the rope.

I do not know of a rim to river route near Tiger Wash although Harvey Butchart has completed such a route near the ravine at Mile 21.[17] The walk downriver on top of the Redwall in this section of Marble Canyon is relatively easy.

It is possible to walk down the bed of Shinumo Wash to the top of the Redwall formation. The Bureau of Reclamation improved a trail into Shinumo Wash back during the time of dam surveys in Marble Canyon. The trail stays on the left slope and follows the top of the Redwall down canyon to near river Mile 30.5 where a fork goes to the Colorado. Beyond that, the main trail goes on for several miles and peters out in the area above Redwall Cavern.

Frederick Dellenbaugh named Shinumo Altar and of it he wrote; "It stood up so like a great altar, and, having in my mind the house-building Amerinds who had formerly occupied the country, and who the Pai Utes called Shinumo, I called it Shinumo Altar, the name it now bears."[18] Shinumo Altar overlooks Eminence Break and may be climbed from several different directions. The summit affords nice views of the Marble Canyon area.

South Canyon/Bedrock Canyon

South Canyon has received heavy attention in recent years, and quite a trail now exists down South Canyon to Vasey's Paradise. Stanton found a route out of South Canyon after three of his crew drowned in the Colorado River.[19] The most direct access is down the fault line in Bedrock Canyon to South Canyon, then down the main drainage to the top of the Redwall formation. Upstream from South Canyon hikers can scramble down through the Redwall and head down river to Vasey's Paradise. Vasey's Paradise was named after a botanist friend of J. W. Powell.[20] Spring water cascades a short distance to the river here and many boat parties make this a photographic stop. Vegetation is lush, but beware the poison ivy!

Ten Miles below Vasey's Paradise a Supai butte stands above a bend in the river. This Point Hansborough commemorates Peter Hansborough, a member of the 1889 Stanton river expedition, who along with Henry Richards, the party's cook, drowned near 25 Mile Rapids. His remains were discovered on Stanton's 1890 expedition and buried at the base of the point which now bears his name.[21]

Above House Rock Valley, a trail comes off the Kaibab Plateau into upper South Canyon.[22] A good overnight loop trip would be to head down upper South Canyon, cross over to North Canyon behind the Cocks Comb and hike out to the east rim via upper North Canyon.

Tatahatso Point

The easiest access is off highway 89 on a dirt road heading west from Cedar Ridge. It is about twenty miles out to the end of Tatahatso Point and the old dam survey tramway. Near its end, the road crosses a fault line that provides the easiest way off the rim of Tatahatso Point. This is the head of the Eminence Break route or President Harding route. A fallen Tower of Kaibab limestone bridges the descent ravine and is a good marker for locating the route from above. The route follows the ravine down through the upper formations then stays atop a steep talus to the Supai. There are two routes through the Supai. One can either stay in the main ravine and directly downclimb the various ledges (a rope will be needed to lower packs and perhaps people), or take an obscure cairned track to the left. This alternate route has several variations, but all require passing behind a strange looking erosional knob, called a hoodoo by the geologists. Below, the route works its way down to the Redwall where Tatahatso Wash joins the fault ravine. Climb south out of the Redwall and continue another one half mile to where a trail of use descends rapidly to the river.

A more sporty route off the rim can be found in Tatahatso Wash and an excellent two or three day trek would be to descend to the Redwall Rim via Tatahatso Wash, contour around to the Eminence Break route and then exit that route back to the rim. Harvey Butchart discusses this route in his guides, but essentially one enters the wash where it crosses Eminence Break via the southwest ravine.[23] A rope is handy for lowering packs in the lower Kaibab and Toroweap. There is moderate boulder-hopping in the wash below. Some rough sections are on the Redwall contour especially as one nears the Eminence Break route. Look across the river for the Anasazi bridge at about Mile 43.3.[24]

Saddle Canyon

Coming off the rim, Butchart put in a route down this canyon to the top of the Redwall, but there is a 100 foot rappel through the Coconino Sandstone. This is where he hung upside down in his etriers while re-ascending his rope and ended up hiking clear around into Nankoweap on an all night death march to get back to his vehicle.[25]

You can reach the base of the Redwall from the river, but there is no route through the Redwall. There is however, a scramblers route at Mile 49.9 which will provide a rim to river passage. The top part of this route is vari-

11

ously referred to as the "Boundary Ridge Route," "Eminence Point Route," or the "Graham-Mitchell Route" (after Dale Graham and Ron Mitchell who first notified Harvey Butchart of its possibilities). This steep and somewhat dangerous route leaves the rim in a bay on the north side of the extreme eastern end of Boundary Ridge. A striking mushroom like tower of Kaibab limestone signals the correct place to start. Ropes are warranted, especially if hikers stay overnight. Several routes through the Coconino (at least three) get one down into the main fault ravine. The Supai is easy, but the Redwall requires some care and a good eye for route finding. Stay to the south side of the Redwall ravine to start.[26]

Sase Nasket

Ohlman saw a possible route back in 1976 and told various people about it. Recently, Glenn Rink and Kenton Grua succeeded in completing a near ropeless route from rim to river at this spot, located across the river from Harvey's Mile 49.9 Redwall route. They used a rope only for protection while ascending from the river. The top part of the route goes up the ravine southeast of Sase Nasket.

Little Nankoweap

It is an easy walk from Nankoweap up the delta along the river to Little Nankoweap. Ohlman and others have climbed up through the Redwall formation in several places in the Little Nankoweap drainage, and hikers can either continue up Little Nankoweap and ascend to Titled Mesa, or exit via one of several Coconino breaks off the east end of Boundary Ridge. The Kaibab poses some route finding problems, so a rope would be handy.

1 Measles (1981) pp. 5-28 [long narrative of Lee's life at the Ferry after the Mountain Meadows Massacre]

2 Brian (1992) p. 12

3 Rusho and Crampton (1975) pp. 63-73 [Spencer apparently lost out on his gold mining venture, because his steamship was incapable of hauling sufficient coal for both itself and the mining operation, and because the gold was too fine for his sluices]; Aitchinson (1985) pp. 61-64

4 *Ibid.,* pp. 10-12 [the padres crossed at a place appropriately named, "Crossing of the Fathers"]

5 *Ibid.,* p. 49 [reference to "Honeymoon Trail"]; Kelsey (1986) pp. 178-179; Butchart (1975) pp. 7-9; Brian (1992) pp. 13, 17, 20 [historic information of the CCC, Echo Peaks, Buzzard Highline and Dugway trails]

6 Aitchinson (1985) p. 70 [Cathedral Wash Route]; q. v. Annerino (1986) p. 277

7 Kelsey (1987) pp. 156-158] this is the most authoritative guide available for hiking within Paria Canyon and Buckskin Gulch. Also covers several routes to the Paria Plateau in House Rock Valley]

8 Aitchinson (1985) pp. 67-69 [CCC trail]

9 Annerino (1986) pp. 277-278; q. v. Aitchinson. (1985) p. 71 [Jackass Canyon]

10 Aitchinson (1985) pp. 72-73 [Soap Creek]; q. v. Butchart (1975) p. 11 also Butchart (1984) p. 9-11 [Brief mention]; Kelsey (1986) pp. 182-183

11 Kelsey (1986) pp. 180-181; Aitchinson (1985) pp. 74-76; Annerino (1986) p. 278

12 Butchart (1975) p. 12

13 Kelsey (1986) pp. 184-185

14 *Ibid.,* pp. 186-187; Aitchinson (1985) pp. 77-80

15 Aitchinson (1985) pp. 77-80 [Road Log pp. 77-79]

16 Rainbow Expeditions (1980) Lee's Ferry Map; Arizona State Parks Association (1990) [refer to section on North Canyon Trail #4]; North Kaibab Guide (N. D.) pp. 20-21 [also covers Forest Service Trails into South Canyon, Nankoweap and Saddle Mountain areas, as well as trails into Kanab Creek and Jumpup Canyon Area]

17 Butchart (1975) pp. 15-16; _____ (N. D.) [q. v. logs for 4/24/66, 5/7/66, 1/4/67, 11/27/70and 12/19/70]; Aitchinson (1985) pp. 81-83

18 Dellenbaugh (1902) p. 310

19 Lavender (1985) pp. 24-25; Smith and Crampton (eds 1987) pp. 65, 82-83, 87-88n, 93n

20 Simmons and Gaskill (1972) p. 46; q. v. Hamblin and Rigby (1968) pp. 39-41 (1968); q. v. Aitchinson (1985) pp. 85-87

21 Lavender (1985) pp. 24, 27; Smith and Crampton (1987) pp. 138-139, 139n

22 North Kaibab Guide (N. D.) pp. 22-23; Arizona State Parks Association (1990) [refer to section on South Canyon Trail #6]

23 Butchart (1975) pp. 17-18; _____ (1984) p. 14

24 Stevens (1983) p. 69; Butchart (1975) pp. 17-18

25 Butchart (1975) pp. 23-24; _____ (1984) p. 13 q. v. Butchart (N. D.) [Trip Logs for 12/20-21/69 and 12/23/69]

26 Butchart (1975) p. 21-22, 24-25

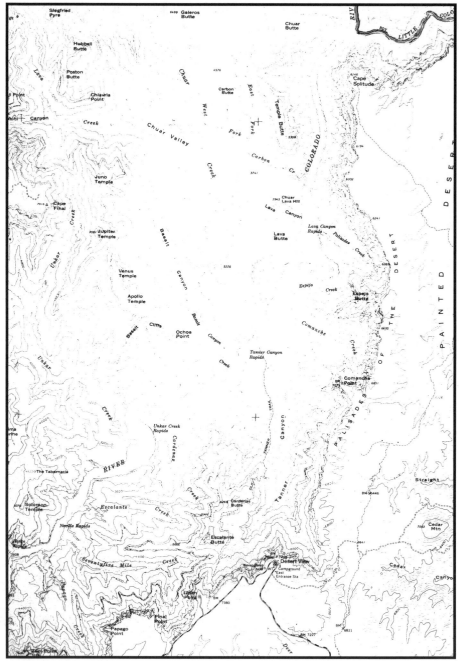

Below the East Rim Drive   *1962 USGS*

Below the East Rim Drive

Little Colorado River

Between Desert View and Cameron off Highway 64 the expanse of the Little Colorado River Gorge may be seen. Walls of this canyon are sheer with drops of 2500-3000 feet in places. The Little Colorado River Canyon has lured many hikers into the gorge and its beauty parallels that of Grand Canyon proper.

Hikers may backpack for many days down the gorge from Cameron on the Navajo Indian Reservation to the confluence with the Colorado River in Grand Canyon. A word of warning, however; the Little Colorado drains a vast portion of northern Arizona and is subject to flash flooding, especially during the spring and mid-late summer. Hikers should understand the risk involved and be prepared to move quickly when the need arises.

Hikers starting up canyon from the confluence will need to cross the sky blue waters of the Little Colorado River many times before reaching the source of permanent water at Blue Springs. Enroute they will pass Ben Beamer's cabin near the confluence, the so called Walter Powell route, the Sipapu and the Hopi Salt Trail. Little Colorado River is much warmer than the Colorado and when not in flood stage presents only a few problems to crossing. Water flows continuously from Blue Springs. The water is highly mineralized, but I have survived on it for a few days at a time without ill effect.

The Walter Powell route lies in the first unnamed canyon up from the confluence on the north side of the Little Colorado River. Stay on the western slope of the drainage after leaving the river, then traverse below the Redwall around a small point into a scree and boulder-filled drainage. The route goes up the left side of the drainage. On top of the Redwall the main drainage leads northeast to the rim. A handline to raise and lower packs is a good idea, especially in the Kaibab. Walter Powell may have used part of this route during the Powell surveys of the Colorado River, hence the name.[1]

The Sipapu is an unusually shaped spring on the north bank of the river, approximately 4.5 miles up from the confluence. It is capped by a conical, yellowish travertine formation and its water is sacred to the Hopi Indians. Upstream of the Sipapu, Salt Trail Canyon enters into the gorge from the north. The Salt Trail (or Hopi Salt Trail) was traversed by the Hopi who would pilgrimage to their salt deposits, located downstream from the confluence with the Colorado River. Although difficult to follow in places, there are a number of large rock cairns to guide the uncertain hiker along the course of the trail.[2]

Farther upstream Butchart, George Billingsley and others have explored routes into upper Big Canyon and Jim Ohlman has made it down to the Little Colorado River using a 40 foot rope at one place in the Redwall.[3]

Looking across from Desert View you can see Cedar Mesa and beyond that Gold Hill. A road going north and east around Gold Hill leads to the western rim of the Gorge and passes very near the Blue Springs Trail at mile 13. Here the government built a trail from the source of the blue water to within a few hundred feet of the rim.[4] The upper section of this trail is rough enough to raise and lower rucksacks with a rope, and at least one hiker has fallen near the Redwall rim, with broken bones as a consequence.

At about mile 21 the "Paiute Trail" will take a backpacker from rim to canyon bottom and up to the opposite rim. The west side ravine is rocky and steep, but the east side ravine contains fragments of an old sheep trail and is easy except for one short ledge near the top.[5] Immediately below this route the drainage bottom of the Little Colorado River is dry. On the east side below the "Paiute Trail" is an old horse trail that was constructed during the 1920's. The lower part is now washed out and impassable to livestock, but hikers should have no trouble here.[6] There are at least five additional trails or routes in the Little Colorado Gorge above Mile 21 and the reader is directed to Butchart's 1965 article for information on these. Other Little Colorado trails are at mile 33.5 (Indian Maid and Moody Trails), Mile 41.3 (Red Butte Wash), Mile 47.5 (Dam Site Trail) Mile 50 (Hopi Crossing).

The drainage above Blue Springs is dry for the most part except during wet weather or where small ephemeral seeps and springs occur. Sometimes it is possible to find standing pools of water after a flood, but beware of giardia and other nasty water-borne organisms.

16

Tanner Trail

This is a very dry trail with little shade and it is advisable during summer months to start the hike early and avoid the heat of the day. Tanner Trail is about 9 miles in length from rim to river.

Seth Tanner was an early Mormon settler who improved an earlier Indian trail to his copper mines down along the river.[7] Many years ago this was known as the Horsethief Trail. Supposedly, horses were stolen in Utah and taken to Arizona rim to rim using the Nankoweap and Tanner Trails as entry points to the Grand Canyon.[8]

Most hikers start the trip by leaving Lipan Point on its east side. There are some rock cairns to follow and the Park Service has erected a trailhead sign a little way south and east of the Point. The trail cuts a short distance thru the cedars (junipers) then begins to switchback down a steep

Desert View Watchtower.
The structure was designed during the
1930's by Mary Jane Colter. It is
operated by the Fred Harvey Company.
Photo By: G. Langdale, 1944.

Section of Harvey Butchart's hiking map; Desert View area west to Horshoe Mesa.
Over a period of 50 years, Butchart hiked some 20,000 miles in Grand Canyon.
Photo By: M. Quinn, NPS.   Grand Canyon National Park #12780

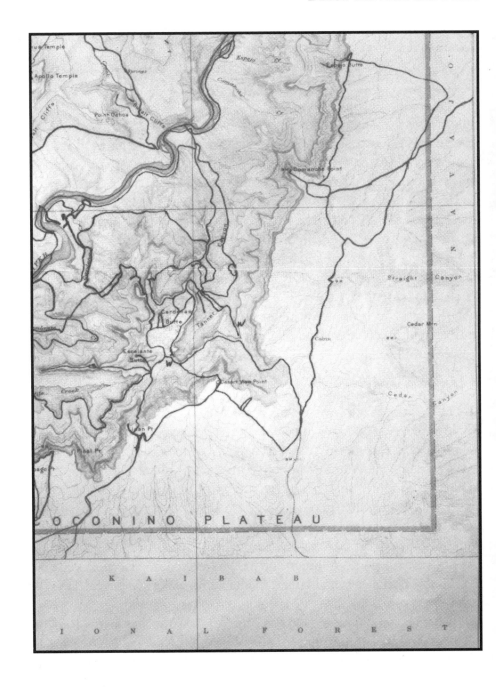

side canyon. Rockslides have knocked out several sections of the trail in the Coconino Sandstone and hikers must follow rock cairns.

The trail reaches the 75 Mile Canyon saddle with some spectacular views of the Grand Canyon to the west. Hikers must stay to the east below the saddle to continue on the trail. There are usually rock cairns to follow here, although few are needed.

Butchart has described an alternate way to the Tanner Trail via the Redwall valley to the east, however I found this much more time consuming and there is inadequate parking across the canyon bay from the Watchtower. You may hike this very faint trail on a day hike by staying below the Watchtower on top of the Redwall bench. Across the bay from Desert View there are signs of old trail construction.[9]

Past the saddle the main trail continues along the top of the Redwall below Escalante and Cardenas Buttes, both of which are easy 3rd-4th class climbs. If you begin to get a spectacular view of the canyon while still on top of the Redwall Formation, you missed the Redwall descent; double back and find the trail descending east through the limestone. The trail follows a ridge crest below the Tapeats.

Once I was bitten by a rattlesnake here in the Cambrian rock and had to walk out while my limb was beginning to swell. After taking several hours to hike up to Lipan Point, I went to the clinic on the South Rim. There wasn't a whole lot that could be done, other than suffer for the next ten days. Day four seemed to be the worst. Just lucky it happened on the east end of the canyon. I've also had a rattler hit my boot in Parashant Canyon. Didn't think the snake got me at the time, but a day later my limb was sore and swollen. Perhaps the leather in the boot absorbed most of the venom. Rattlesnakes usually aren't overly aggressive, until you step on one! Another time something struck me in the face this time upstream of Parashant. I was following close behind my buddy Ohlman and thought a tree limb had smacked me. Don't know if snakes hang in trees! Perhaps Jim woke one up and it took a swing at me. Two days later the left side of my head was swollen.

There is camping available along the beach at Tanner Canyon Rapids, but there is no shelter from sun nor rain. Tanner Canyon also has no permanent water, so hikers must rely on the Colorado River. Up Tanner Canyon there is a small spring above the Tapeats fall, but it is dangerous to reach and may not be reliable. I have hiked up Tanner Canyon by way of the drainage bottom and found the Redwall impassable. One must bypass the Tapeats fall where a Catholic Priest fell to his death in the late 1950's.[10]

Seth Tanner was a prospector and one of his mines is upstream from here, at Palisades Creek. Some hikers say that the air in the mine is bad (methane).

Hikers may go downstream from Tanner beach to the upper end of Unkar Rapids where a high cliff comes down to the river. There are ruins on top of a hill above the rapid and also across the river on Unkar Delta. At Unkar there are ruins from a village of perhaps 30 inhabitants.[11] Backpackers may continue on to Escalante Canyon by following a trail along the shale ridge west of Cardenas Creek.

The trail upstream of Tanner Canyon is just as well defined as the one downstream. Butchart has described a route out Comanche Creek, and Comanche Point offers one of the most spectacular views anywhere in the park.[12] Palisades Creek does not go without a rope, but Espejo Butte can be reached via a rugged climbers route off the rim, east of the peak. I used a hand line in several places coming off the rim. Once below the rim a traverse to Espejo Butte is most easily done below the saddle.

Where the cliffs come down to the river at Palisades Creek hikers must go up on the Tapeats bench and follow the Beamer Trail. About two thirds of the way along this trail hikers will pass above the Hopi salt mines, accessible from the trail only by rope.[13] Ben Beamer's cabin is near the confluence and it is possible to climb out of the Little Colorado River Gorge to the rim via the Walter Powell route on a day hike from the confluence.

George Steck along with a number of others have walked the left bank of the Colorado River from President Harding Rapids to the confluence. Opposite Malgosa Crest hikers must swim or climb around a cliff that blocks the pathway, and across from Saddle Canyon, hikers must climb quite high to bypass a long section of river cliffs.[14]

Before creation of Glen Canyon Dam, Harvey Butchart floated much of the Colorado River in this area on an air mattress. Now the water is very cold and this is not safe without a dry suit.[15]

21

Cardenas Creek

A trail winds its way along the river from Tanner Canyon Rapids to Red Canyon. This trail is relatively fast and only takes a few hours to cover the distance between the two canyons. The trail climbs up the ridge above Unkar Rapids, contours around over rocky terrain, and then drops into Escalante Creek. From Escalante Creek one follows a rising ramp of Shinumo Quartzite around into 75 Mile Creek. Descend 75 Mile to the river then head downstream to Papago Canyon. A steep climb at the mouth of Papago followed by an equally steep descent gets hikers back to the river where they can boulder hop the remaining distance to Red Canyon and the start of the Tonto Trail.[16]

Hikers have succeeded in climbing up the Redwall between the twin points northwest of Cardenas Butte. This route, known locally as the "Grandma Spit Trail," breaks through the Tapeats northwest of the Redwall ravine. From the top of the Redwall it seems easiest to climb up to the saddle between Cardenas Butte and Escalante Butte before connecting with the Tanner Trail. The most difficult section of this route is the steep slope below the Tapeats cliff.

One can hardly write a guidebook without including Don Lopez de Cardenas, who discovered the Grand Canyon in the summer of 1540. Some historians believe he and his scouting party were led by Indian guides to the rim of the Canyon somewhere in the vicinity of Lipan Point. Others think the first viewing of Grand Canyon by a white man took place farther west, near Prospect Canyon and the Aubrey Rim. In either case none of the Spaniards succeeded in reaching the river, and for over 300 years thereafter the Grand Canyon was treated as a barrier to travel rather a place to explore.[17]

75 Mile Creek

Several ways off the rim into 75 Mile Creek exist. The easiest leaves Tanner Trail at Lipan Point/Escalante Butte saddle, drops a short distance down the east tributary of 75 Mile then contours around atop of the Redwall on the south side of the canyon. Another way down to the Redwall is south of Lipan Point. The route through the Redwall is on the promontory between

Pinal Point and Lipan Point. Having a rope is handy. A route through the Tapeats is west of the Redwall route.

Red Canyon Trail

Over the last few decades this trail has seen increased activity and every year I find the trail easier to follow. This is not to say that the "New Hance Trail," as it is commonly referred, is easy by any standard. Red Canyon is usually the third or fourth trail that a hiker will hike in Grand Canyon after starting off with initial trips down the South Kaibab, Bright Angel and perhaps the Grandview or Hermit. Red Canyon Trail is washed out in several places, but if hikers take their time they can safely negotiate a way through boulders and scree.

It is about eight miles from rim to river via the New Hance Trail. John Hance built this trail in the 1890's to access his mines along the river. His original trail went down Hance Canyon to the west, but was repeatedly washed out. He relocated his trail in Red Canyon.[18]

Parking for the trail is at Moran Point, from which one must walk back west on the highway approximately 1-1/4 miles where several "No Parking" signs denote the trailhead.

The trail drops off the rim to near the saddle of Coronado Butte, then follows the drainage down to the top of the Redwall formation. After a short but rugged traverse on top of the cliff, the trail drops sharply through the Redwall. It then sidehills the Bright Angel Shale dropping into Red Canyon after passing a drainage coming in from the east. Easy boulder-hopping will take one to the river. Rock choked Hance Rapid is the main attraction, but it is so loud, that I had problems sleeping on the sandy beach next to the river.

I have used my small inflatable raft to cross above Hance Rapids. On the north side there is a trail that leads up to several asbestos mines and there is an unusual rock cairn and inscriptions farther up. Above one of the mines lies an old aircraft wing. Back on the southside of the Colorado River the Tonto Trail begins a 90 mile trek though Grand Canyon ending just beyond Bass Trail.

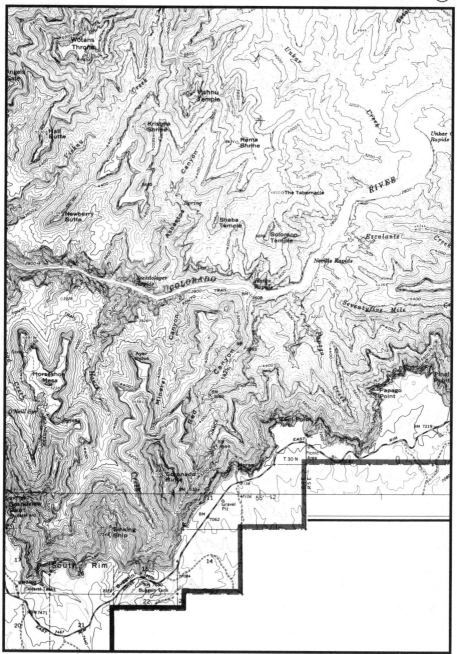

Red Canyon or "New Hance" Area.

1962 USGS

Hance Asbestos Mine.
1958 NPS

Grand Canyon National Park #3495

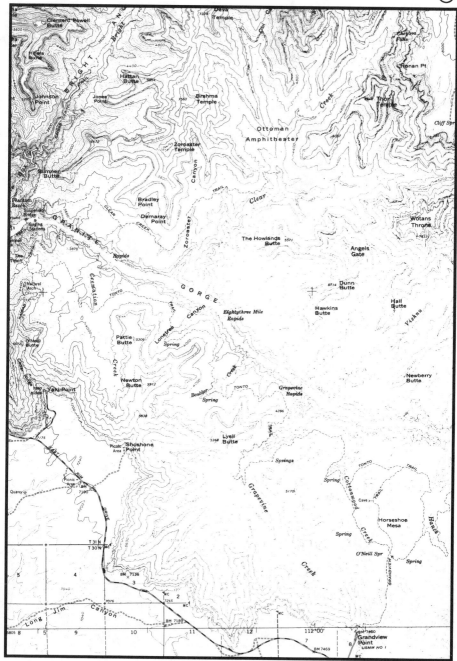

Grandview to Cremation

1962 USGS

26

Grandview Trail

Built in 1895-97, there is nothing left now of the Grandview Hotel.[19] During building of Desert View Watchtower in the 1930's, timbers were taken from the old hotel near Grandview Point and used for rafters in the Tower.[20] During it's heyday, Grandview was the most frequented area of Grand Canyon by tourists. Another hotel near Buggeln Hill now only shows faint traces of a foundation.[21]

Grandview is one of the most scenic trailheads at Grand Canyon. In 1890, a mining claim was filed and construction of the trail began in 1892.[22] Built by miners, the present trail leaves the rim from the northern end of Grandview Point Parking Area. The top section of the trail is steep, and switchbacks were built through the Kaibab and Toroweap Formations. No longer shown on the map, the original trail leaves the rim near the old hotel site south and east of the Grandview parking area and it meets with the popular trail before the Toroweap saddle. The trail winds around a small unnamed peak before making a descent thru the white sandstone. Much work was put into the trail where it makes a drop thru the Coconino Sandstone as evidenced by the cut and placed rock paving stones and log cribbing. From the saddle, below the Coconino Sandstone it is possible to scramble down a rough route into the Hance Canyon drainage. The trail gradually makes its way thru the Supai formation down to Horseshoe Mesa.

There is a trail junction on Horseshoe Mesa near remains of an old cabin. The trail to the right passes by the Last Chance Mine enroute to its connection with the Tonto Trail on the east side of the mesa. There are many levels to the mine and it is quite deep. Mining relics are still evident; including an ore cart with metal track. Hikers should take care when entering the mine because many parts of the shaft are unstable. Miner's Spring is a good source of water for hikers continuing over to Red Canyon.

The trail to the left drops down into Cottonwood Creek where it connects with the Tonto Trail on the west side of Horseshoe Mesa. Cottonwood Creek is a permanent water source. The main trail continues out to the west arm of the Horseshoe where it drops down to meet the Tonto Trail, north of the mesa. The small red butte to the east of the main trail is awkwardly referred to as "Horseshoe Mesa Butte," and was undoubtedly climbed by miners prior to the turn of the century.[23]

27

Horseshoe Mesa is rather famous for caves, but due to heavy vandalism by insensitive tourists, these caves are no longer publicized. Persons desiring to visit Grand Canyon caves should contact the backcountry office for special permits. Mines too are abundant and should be entered and explored only by knowledgeable persons with proper equipment. Note that caves and mines, as well as archeological and historical sites are protected by Federal Law, and nothing may be collected or disturbed without the requisite permits and authorization. As the adage goes: "Take nothing but photographs, leave nothing but footprints."

Across Cottonwood Creek to the west, there is a route through the Redwall, remnants of an old pack trail. Wayne Baker showed me the location of some mescal pits on top of the Redwall near that trail. The Grandview Trail has a spur to the river. This spur does not go down Cottonwood Canyon, but leaves the Tonto Trail on the promontory west of the mouth of Cottonwood Creek. This section of the Grandview Trail is no longer on the map and I have used it to cross with my inflatable raft into Vishnu Canyon on the northside of the Colorado River.

Farther south, there are several Redwall routes into Cottonwood Canyon from the trail. Slim Stout did the southernmost and hardest one, using a rope to descend. I completed two routes south of where the trail comes down from Horseshoe Mesa; neither required a rope however.

You may come into Hance Creek from the Rim several ways, the easiest being the rugged, washed out "Old Hance Trail." Now gone, and not shown on the map, this trail left the rim southeast of Sinking Ship and east of Buggeln Hill. Captain John Hance was a miner, and was in the vicinity of Flagstaff as early as November of 1869. He built a number of trails in Grand Canyon and is buried near the visitor center at Grand Canyon Village.[24]

I have climbed Sinking Ship, and received a cut worth 10 stitches when trying to scramble down into Hance Creek below. Hikers should be aware of the loose footing in the area of the Old Hance Trail.

From atop the Redwall in Hance Canyon it is possible to scramble up to the saddle of Coronado Butte and the Red Canyon Trail. I have climbed Coronado Butte and there is getting to be quite a register on the summit.

Farther down Hance Canyon, Laura Fisher and I followed the Tonto Trail a short distance to the east and were able to climb up through the Redwall on the west side of Ayer Point at its saddle. In 1881, E. E. Ayer from Chicago received the contract to supply ties and other lumber to the railroad, and he built a sawmill near San Francisco Mountain.[25] It is also possible to continue to the river down Hance Canyon, but at least three falls in the creek must be bypassed by climbing up, over and around them.[26]

Grapevine Canyon

The most common access to this canyon is via the Tonto Trail be-
tween the Kaibab and Grandview Trails. On the east side of the canyon there are springs along the trail. Between the springs and where the Tonto crosses Grapevine there is a break in the Tapeats that allows hikers access to the lower canyon. Not too many people venture down here, as the canyon is still relatively pristine, and there is water in the stream bottom. Before reaching the river one must bypass a high fall by climbing east up over a saddle. I have crossed the Colorado River from the north above Vishnu Canyon and used the lower Grapevine Canyon route to return to the Tonto on the southside.

The ravine in the Coconino Sandstone below Grandview Trail leads down into Grapevine Canyon. A fall in the Redwall must be bypassed, but a strong hiker will have little trouble finding his way down here. The fall is bypassed on the right with a little hand and toe climbing. Below the Muav a faint trail on the talus avoids brush in the drainage. J. H. Butchart was most impressed by a stand of redbud trees here and made a note of it in his "Grand Canyon Treks."[27]

To the west Lyell Butte can be climbed via a route off Shoshone Point, but there is no way through the Redwall on that side of Grapevine. Jim Ohlman and I also explored the southwest fork and concluded there was no way up there either.

Above the southernmost arm of Grapevine Canyon, Wayne Baker showed me some old Indian Paintings under an overhang. There was what appeared to be a map drawn on the overhang showing a route off Shoshone into Cremation Canyon, a route down the southernmost arm of Grapevine and another comes into Grapevine from Grandview Point. My first trip down the southernmost arm of Grapevine was a route Wayne Baker had described to me. I ventured past the chockstone in the Coconino sandstone but was stopped by a fall in the Supai. On my second trip I found a

29

bypass to that fall. With a late start that day, it was dusk by the time I had found a route through the Supai cliffs. In the drainage I came to a high fall in the Redwall. Traversing to the west, I did a series of rappels from ledge to ledge. Darkness overtook me on the last rappel, but I was below the Redwall. After retrieving the doubled rope I carefully, with a flashlight in hand, made a way down the drainage to the Tonto Trail. On a third trip with Jim Ohlman, we were able to find a ropeless route down the Redwall east of the large pouroff, and completed the route without much difficulty to the Tonto Trail.

Shoshone Point

My interest in this area started in 1979 when Wayne Baker showed me the location of some storage granaries below the rim. He also had succeeded in going off the rim to the Tonto Trail in Cremation Canyon, and found worn Anasazi hand and foot holds in the Coconino Sandstone.

A deer trail in a bay south of Shoshone Point gets hikers through the Kaibab limestone. A Toroweap cliff is passed on the west side of the point and the route through the Coconino goes down the ridge, north below Shosone Point. At a difficult section in the Coconino you must descend where the cliff is broken on the east side. There are places a man must lower his rucksack.

From the Hermit Shale you can climb Lyell Butte by going down the tributary to the east. It is also possible to go down the Hermit ridge to the saddle south of Newton Butte. I have failed twice to climb Newton. Pattie Butte is only a little harder to climb than Lyell and if a hiker can come down Shosone Point he most certainly has the ability to climb Pattie Butte. This peak was named after James Ohio Pattie, an early trapper.[28]

From the Shoshone/Newton saddle you may go through the Redwall to the west and access Cremation Creek. One December I broke my flashlight while coming down into Cremation. I had finished a day hike and now could not locate my camp in Cremation Canyon. I searched and searched in the darkness, finally finding the sleeping bag well after midnight. Another Redwall route into Cremation is located behind a pinnacle, west and south of the Newton/Pattie saddle.

 1 Butchart (1976) p. 40; Brian (1992) p. 44
 2 Butchart (1965a); Brian (1992) p. 44
 3 Butchart (1970) pp. 35-38; Ohlman [12/3/94 and 1/5/95], Butchart (N. D.) [logs for
    6/1-3/90 and 3/14/92] (N. D.) [logs for 9/22/73, 1/19/74]
 4 Butchart (1965a); q. v.; Wing (1956) [Describes a hike/float trip from Blue Springs to the
    Colorado River and out via the Tanner Trail]
 5 U. S. Geological Survey (1926); Butchart (1965a) p. 41
 6 *Ibid.*
 7 Hughes (1978) p. 53; Brian (1992) p. 50; Spangler (1986) pp. 123-124
 8 Butchart (1976) pp. 37-39; Brian (1992) p. 50; Hughes (1978) p. 53; James (1900) pp.
    244-246
 9 Butchart (1976) p. 37
10 Butchart (1976) p. 38
11 Schwartz, *et al* (1980); Butchart (1976) p. 57
12 Butchart (1984) pp. 19-22
13 Spangler (1986) pp. 124-125; Butchart (1965a) pp. 34-35, 38
14 Ohlman (N. D.) [log for 10/18-21/91]
15 Butchart (1960) [Entire article concerns using an air mattress on the river for purposes of
    accessing areas of the canyon]
16 Annerino (1986) pp. 198-201
17 Hughes (1978) pp. 19-20; Annerino (1986) pp. 173-174; Brian (1992) pp. 51-52
18 *Ibid.,* pp. 47, 49; Sutphen (1992c) [Historical perspective of John Hance and his trails]
19 Good (1985) pp. 17-21; Spangler (1986) p. 25; Hughes (1978) pp. 54-55
20 1981 interpretive talk, Desert View
21 Hughes (1978) p. 50
22 Good (1985) pp. 7-12; Butchart (1976) p. 30; Sutphen (1991a); q. v. Sutphen (1991b)
23 q. v. Annerino (1986) p. 213
24 Sutphen (1992c); Hughes (1978) pp. 47-50; Garrison (1949); Brian (1992) pp. 55-57
25 Hughes (1978) pp. 48-49; q. v. Brian (1992) p. 56
26 Butchart (1976) p. 35 [discusses route to river]
27 Butchart (1976) p. 30
28 Brian (1992) p. 60

Topo map of Grand Canyon between Pt. Imperial and Cape Royal. There are over 150 named peaks in Grand Canyon; mostly in the eastern part of the park.

Courtesy of Arizona Strip District Bureau of Land Management.

Below the Walhalla Plateau

Nankoweap Trail

Charles Walcott, a geologist with Powell's Survey, improved an old Indian route into Nankoweap basin in 1882. This unmaintained trail is waterless except for the last mile and a half where it follows Nankoweap Creek down to the Colorado River. It has a southern exposure for most of the way and there is little shade. This 14 mile trail has two access trailheads. Coming up out of House Rock Valley, south of the Buffalo Ranch, one trail makes its way up upper Saddle Canyon to the saddle between Saddle Mountain and the North Rim. Another trail comes in off the North Rim at the end of Forest/Park Boundary road (FS 610). In many places this trail is vague and a hiker should stay on the north side of the ridge to avoid cliffs. Both access trails converge at the saddle west of Saddle Mountain to form the Nankoweap Trail proper.[1]

From the junction of the two trails hikers have climbed Saddle Mountain and enjoyed the views of Marble Canyon and eastern Grand Canyon from its summit. Saddle Mountain is often wind swept and the trees show frost damage.

The Nankoweap Trail drops below the saddle to the south and begins a long traverse along red Supai formation. Many parts are washed out, and there is at least one narrow spot where the trail has fallen away.

When attempting to climb to Marion Point, I found an easy scramble down to its saddle from the trail. An elongated peak, Marion, is one of the easiest Grand Canyon summits to climb. Climbers have also been up the west side of Barbenceta Butte, a long walk beyond where the trail drops off Tilted Mesa. An 8 foot high cliff is breached by a crack on its south side. There is loose rock at the top of this route.

There may be some confusion where the trail is located in the Redwall, but if a hiker takes his time he can reach the canyon floor without too much difficulty. In general, when in doubt, head southeastward toward a noticeable slump of Redwall limestone. The trail does not cut back to the north, nor does it head straight down below Tilted Mesa.[2]

33

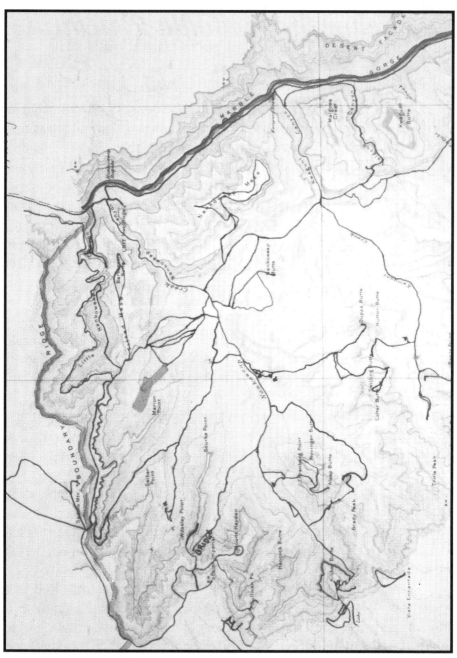

Butcharts hike map; J.H. Butchart has climbed over 80 peaks in Grand Canyon.
Photo By: M. Quinn, 1994, NPS   Grand Canyon National Park #12,779

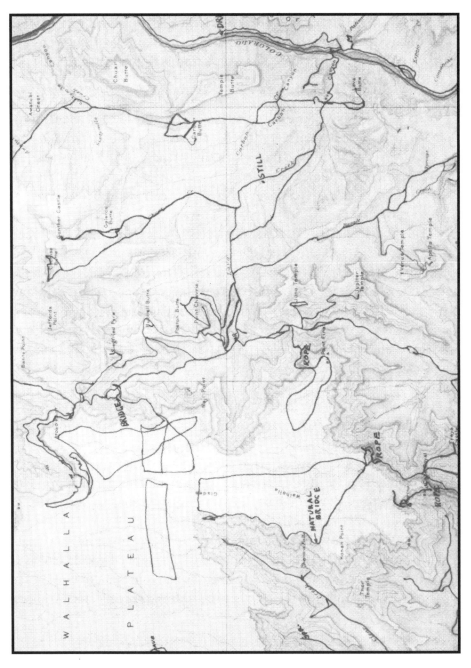

Nankoweap Mesa is climbed on its west side by ascending the white cliffs where they are broken above the saddle. Nankoweap Butte is an easy climb, and is the only Grand Canyon summit capped by the younger precambrian Sixty Mile formation.

After the trail reaches Nankoweap Creek, it is an easy walk down to the Colorado River. Above the delta some Indian ruins are located under a cliff. Some of the earliest written records about natives in the area are those of the Kwagunts. The brother lived on the east side of the Kaibab Plateau and has a canyon named after him here in the Nankoweap area. His sister lived on the west side of the Plateau, there being a small side canyon named after her in Kanab Canyon.[3]

The "Horsethief Trail" starts where Nankoweap Trail meets the creek bed and crosses the saddle between Nankoweap Butte and Mesa. Horses were stolen in Utah and a transcanyon trail system allowed thieves to move horses into Flagstaff for sale.[4] Most certainly this was done at low water and not in the early spring. The Horsethief Trail continued down canyon toward the Tanner Trail by "saddle hopping" west of Nankoweap into Kwagunt, and successively from there into Malgosa, Awatubi, Sixty Mile, Carbon and finally into Chuar/Lava Creek, where it crossed the Colorado River near Lava Canyon Rapids.

You may use calm water above Lava Canyon Rapids to cross with a small inflatable raft, and Chuar Canyon is an easy walk down the saddle fault line.

Farther up Nankoweap drainage, Slim Stout and I have climbed Kibbey Butte and there is a precarious route down to Nankoweap Creek from the saddle of the peak. The route off the rim to the red shale is very brushy. Wearing a thick long sleeve shirt helps.

B. J. Boyle showed me a route north of Point Imperial that leads down to the Hermit shale. The slope is brushy, but climbers use this route to access Mount Hayden. While flying over the canyon, Senator Goldwater discovered a natural bridge (Kolb) between Mount Hayden and Woolsey Butte.[5]

Kwagunt Creek

It is an easy walk up from the Colorado River into Kwagunt Valley. Hikers may also come over the saddle between Nankoweap Mesa and Nankoweap Butte. Kwagunt Creek has a perennial flow and I have camped in the Valley for several days drinking its water.

The Butte Fault is a major fracture in the earths crust, whose surface expression is a series of saddles and upturned sedimentary beds visible along a linear path, west of the six great buttes, and extending from Nankoweap Creek south to Lava Canyon and beyond. One can easily follow this faultline out of Kwagunt over into Nankoweap Valley, and I have followed the break into Lava Canyon, climbing Lava Butte near its south end.

Nankoweap Mesa may be climbed on its west side and Nankoweap Butte from several directions. Bruce Grubbs and Larry Trieber are credited with the first ascent of Malgosa Crest, via a route on its south side.[6] Ohlman, Kirschvink and Smith made the first ascent of Hutton Butte in 1981.[7] Duppa Butte is climbed easily on its southern ridge; Colter Butte from east or west. Swilling Butte was climbed by a route on it's east side by a team of climbers led by Butchart in 1973.[8] Kwagunt Butte is the most technically difficult summit to reach in the entire eastern Grand Canyon. The only known route is on its west end and holds a rating of III, 5.9(A.2)1. Grubbs, Trieber, Abbink and Haggart are credited with the first ascent.[9]

Awatubi Crest may be climbed rather easily from its saddle. Here strata was uplifted and layers of rock are nearly vertical instead of horizontal. Farther south I was stopped by a high fall in the Redwall above Sixty Mile Canyon, but Packard, Walters and others have succeeded in reaching the Butte Fault from the river.

A route goes through the Redwall just west of Banta Point and you can climb to the rim from the Hermit shale via a deer trail southwest of Atoko Point. Other Redwall routes exist on the west side of Jeffords Point; in the ravine immediately east of Point Atoko; and at the head of Kwagunt Valley in the main bed. All of these routes require scrambling skills.

You may walk along the Colorado River between Nankoweap Creek and Chuar Butte. Near the Chuar Butte/Temple Butte saddle I climbed up onto a bench above the river to continue south, then hiked into Chuar West Fork above the Carbon Creek gorge. Jim Kirschvink found a route down Carbon Creek and was able to make his way along the river to just short of Chuar Creek and a river crossing.

Chuar

It is an easy walk up Chuar Creek from the Colorado River and there is reliable water in Chuar Creek. Perhaps the easiest peak to climb in this section of Grand Canyon is Chuar Lava Hill which is climbed from the ridge above Carbon Creek. Lava Butte is a little harder and it has a chimney crack on its south side. Carbon Butte is easy, but remote. There is a great deal of freedom to move about in the Chuar Valley and it is not like most places in Grand Canyon.

The climb of Temple Butte is on its northwestern face and the Redwall break here is quite steep. Grubbs and Haggart climbed Temple Butte as early as 1978.[10] The area between Temple Butte and Chuar Butte still contains wreckage from an 1956 mid-air collision of two aircraft. Most of the remaining wreckage lies on the river side of the peaks.[11]

Gunther Castle may be climbed via a ravine in the Redwall on its south side. The ravine is not too difficult, just some scrambling up the drainage. Above the Redwall a route weaves through the Supai cliffs utilizing scree slopes. Butchart, Davis, Doty and Ellis climbed Gunther in 1969.[12] On a climb of Gunther in 1981 Ohlman, Kirschvink and Smith found an old survey tripod at the summit. Perhaps Matthes and Evans, early canyon mappers, used Gunther for a triangulation station during their survey.[13]

There is a small unnamed Peak between Galeros and Hubbell Butte that I was able to climb from the west. Someday mappers may get around to naming the summit. Galeros Butte is moderate 3rd or 4th class on the north side of its eastern ridge. Cochise Butte can be climbed from either the east or west, and from either Kwagunt Creek (harder) or Chuar West Fork (best).

Ohlman, Kirschvink and I climbed Chuar Butte via the saddle and a rugged technical route on the northwest side. There is a deep ravine here with a cliff that is quite steep. Luckily I was roped up when a hand hold broke and Ohlman was able to hold me on belay. From the summit there are spectacular views of the Little Colorado River and sky blue water. Only brush grows on top of Chuar Butte and wildlife seems to be limited to birds, lizards and mice. After some summit photos and lunch we rappeled back down to the slopes above the valley, using bolts placed in the rock by a prior ascent party. The first recorded ascent of Chuar Butte was in 1978 by Grubbs and Haggart; but Melvin McCormick, an old-timer whose father once ran the Tanner Copper Mines, said that he and a friend climbed Chuar back in 1910's-1920's.[14]

Unlike the solid granite of Yosemite, rock in Grand Canyon is often the consistency of dirt clods. Bushes in most cases are more solid than crud rock around them. Talus, weathered cracks, hand holds that break away and insecure anchors are common rule in the Grand Canyon and require a subtle approach when climbing.

Archaeologists have located a few sites at Chuar Creek and perhaps the Indians who lived at Unkar delta camped here on their way to Salt Trail Canyon.

There are several routes commonly used to access Chuar from the North Rim. One route leaves the rim west of Atoko Point then winds its way around the red Hermit shale to the saddle of the peak with elevation 7685. A second route leaves the rim 3/4 mile north of Naji Point and descends via a steep ravine to the Redwall above Hartman Bridge. Both Routes are useful to climbers heading for Siegfried, Hubbell and Poston Buttes, or for those wishing to reach the permanent water in Lava Canyon. Each route has its drawbacks, however. The Point Atoko route is unbelievably brushy. While the Hartman Bridge direct route requires a rope or handline in the Coconino and brush can be a problem for those who stray off course.

Most Grand Canyon climbers prefer the spring and fall for their adventures. The summer temperatures become extreme and winter time weather is unpredictable. A pair of climbers trying to set a record for the number of climbs during a certain length of time were caught in a November snow storm below the North Rim. In a fogout below Siegfried Pyre visibility was so poor that one of the climbers later stated he could hold a hand out at arms' length and not see his fingers. With erroneous judgment they hiked out Atoko Point and "post holed" through snow for parts of three days to House Rock Valley. Not prepared for a storm, one climber suffered frostbite of the feet. Fortunately, this hiker can still count all ten toes and an indelible lesson was learned.

From Lava Creek I climbed Hubbell Butte via a small canyon west of the peak. Poston Butte is easy from Hubbell and there is a break in the Redwall going east from the Poston/Chiavaria saddle. Poston and Hubbell were climbed as early as 1963 by Butchart and Springorum.[15] Siegfried was first climbed by Donald Davis and Robbie Babb via a ravine on its southwest end.[16] A near record pinyon pine once struggled for existence atop Siegfried, but recent news has it this tree lost its battle.

Harvey Butchart put in a rope route off the North Rim in a ravine northwest of Cape Final, however I have not yet attempted it.[17] Jim Ohlman has climbed out the Cape Final route (rope needed for safety) and noted some cut moqui steps along the way. There is a rugged scramble down the Redwall north of the Cape Final/Juno saddle into Natchi Canyon. A Tapeats fall is bypassed along a terrace to the west. Juno Temple is an easy climb from the Chuar/Unkar saddle.

*Rock slide below
Ochoa Point.*

Basalt Creek Canyon

There are some alkali seeps in Basalt Canyon Creek, but the water is bitter. During one long summer day I was able to cross the Colorado River on my little inflatable raft from Cardenas Creek to Basalt Canyon, climb Venus and Apollo Temples and return to Cardenas on the southside. It is not difficult to walk up to the level of the Tonto in this canyon and there are several ways over the ridge that divides Chuar from Basalt. Hikers with a little care in route finding should not encounter any problems going over the hump. There are old relics from the days miners were in the canyon and it is interesting to poke around in the old prospects. Take the eastern fork in Basalt to avoid some cliffs of Cardenas lavas.

It would be interesting to attempt to climb Jupiter Temple from the Basalt Canyon side someday. I have climbed Ochoa Point from both north and south. The climb seemed much harder than that of Apollo and Venus because it was the middle of the summer and temperatures were soaring to over 100 degrees. Venus and Apollo Temples are usually climbed via a Redwall canyon on their east side, and there may be a possible route on the south end of Apollo. J. H. Butchart climbed both these peaks in 1965.[18]

One can walk along the river from Basalt Canyon to Unkar Creek, but there are narrow ledges along part of the way. However, the route on the south side of the river seems much faster when hiking from Tanner Canyon Rapids to Unkar Creek Rapids.

Unkar Creek

Unkar Creek delta contains a number of ancient Indian ruins from a village which was home to perhaps as many as thirty people. Douglas Schwartz excavated the delta and wrote a book on his findings.[19]

Unkar Creek has a trickle of a stream on the lower end and additional springs may be found higher up. Climb Juno Temple from the delta via the Unkar/Chuar saddle. During hot weather this peak becomes challenging indeed.

Tom Furgason and Jim Ohlman climbed Juno, Jupiter, Venus and Apollo Temples all on one long dayhike off the north rim.[20] The Jupiter/Venus saddle is treacherous, but one could get through the Redwall in the ravine west of this saddle. Hikers can also climb up to the saddle between Freya Castle and Vishnu Temple via several ravines.

West of the delta the Tapeats formation is weathered enough to allow hikers passage to the Tonto Platform. I have climbed The Tabernacle by this route. Solomon and Sheba Temples can also be accessed from a camp in lower Unkar.

Vishnu

The easiest way to access Vishnu Creek is via Grandview Trail from the South Rim. The water is glassy smooth above Vishnu Canyon and I have found my light weight backpack raft with a life preserver safe enough to do the crossing. Note, however that you must land in a small bay above the mouth of Vishnu. Continuing around this Red Granite spit and into the mouth is inviting disaster! You can reach a camp atop the Tonto in Vishnu in one day from the south rim using this route. Alternate methods involve several days walking from Bright Angel and Clear Creeks.

Another route that Harvey Butchart has described leaves the rim of Cape Royal, southeast of the ruins located on the map. This is the most rugged access into Vishnu Creek and Slim Stout and I encountered difficulty finding the correct slot in the Coconino Sandstone.[21] Using a handline on a steep slab helped us get close enough to the edge of a cliff to see a small ledge leading down to the right. Its not much of a step, but having a handline is a help and from the ledge the rest of the descent to Hermit shale is easy.

The first recorded ascent of Vishnu Temple was done by Merrell Clubb and his son Roger during the summer of 1946.[22] This summit is one of the most prominent geographic features in eastern Grand Canyon and it can be seen for many miles both up and downriver. Ironically, Merrell Clubb's son and grandson were killed in a flash flood at Indian Garden: being swept away near where the Park Service posts a flash flood warning sign along Bright Angel Trail.[23]

Slim Stout and I were able to climb Freya Castle via a Coconino slide on the east side. Butchart describes a route up Wotans Throne which ascends a ravine on the southeast side of the Cape Royal/Wotans saddle then traverses around to the northside and climbs up through the Kaibab

Slim Stout on a difficult section below Cape Royal. The route is used by climbers on their way to Wotans Throne.

limestone near the west end.[24] After climbing Freya Castle Slim Stout and I gave up our attempt to climb Wotans Throne and returned to the rim.

You can climb up through the Redwall in Vishnu Canyon via several ways. A small canyon leading up to the Vishnu/Freya saddle allowed me to climb Krishna Shrine from the north. The Cape Royal/Freya saddle goes but there is a Supai cliff that must be bypassed in order to reach Freya and Wotan.

While climbing up a chimney crack on Krishna Shrine I came face to face with a rattlesnake some twenty five feet up a cliff. Luckily it was shy and went farther back into a crack. After attaining the summit I made my way down farther east to avoid another encounter! The Redwall ravine north of the Vishnu/Krishna saddle is faster, but a ravine south of Krishna is safer. Krishna Shrine was first climbed by Harvey Butchart in 1962, and peak X5650 has also had teams of climbers.[25] Krishna can also be approached via Redwall ravines to both the north and south. The Vishnu/Freya saddle also allows

43

hikers access into Unkar Creek. Hall Butte is easily climbed from the east and there is a small muddy seep above the Tapeats along the way. From Hall one can also continue on to Hawkins Butte along the top of the Redwall, but that's a long day round trip from Vishnu Creek. You may walk the top of the Redwall here for a short cut back to Clear Creek, but a rope is needed on the west side of Wotans Throne/Angels Gate saddle.

Newberry, Sheba and Solomon are all climbed on their east side. Newberry was the most difficult of the three for me. Queen Sheba and King Solomon are described in the Old Testament. Newberry was a geologist on the 1858 Ives Expedition across Arizona. He was also a surgeon and a naturalist. Newberry's geologic reports were a major advancement in the study of northern Arizona.[26] Except for a spring in Asbestos Canyon, the Tonto Platform is dry between Vishnu and Unkar Creeks.

You can climb Rama Shrine from the south via a Redwall canyon that leads out of Asbestos Canyon; it takes one long summer's day to make this summit from the Hance mines and return. Carrying two gallons of water helped beat dehydration, but the extra weight took its toll. The Supai formation can be passed on either the east side or southwest ridge. There is a natural arch visible from near the summit that is not shown on the map. In an interpretation of the Bhagavad-Gita, A. C. Bhaktivedanta Swami Prabhupada defined Rama as a name of Lord Krishna meaning "the source of all pleasure"; and also Lord Ramachandra, an incarnation of Krishna as a perfect righteous king. Rama also is Hindu for "prince." Vishnu becomes the redeemer, Krishna the 8th incarnation of Vishnu and Rama the Avatar of Vishnu.[27]

The Tabernacle is an easy climb and it is possible to drop into Unkar Creek from east of the summit. Another route off the Tonto into Unkar lies east of Rama Shrine.

West of Newberry Butte there are several routes in the Tapeats that take hikers from the Tonto to the bottom of Vishnu Creek. The scramble down the precambrian rock is not too difficult. Below the Tonto, east of Newberry Butte a trail, no longer shown on the map, leads down to the Hance asbestos mines and the Colorado River. Despite the lack of use, this trail remains in relatively good condition today. One mine shows rather extensive work on it. Hance developed a river crossing from the foot of this trail into

44

Red Canyon for the purpose of hauling his ore out to the South Rim. There is a spring in Asbestos Canyon and a ravine southwest of Sheba Temple leads up to the Tonto Platform with little difficulty.

1 Aitchinson (1985) pp. 88-91; Kaibab National Forest (N. D.) pp. 30-31 [Nankoweap Trail #57]; Kelsey (1986) pp. 250-254
2 Aitchinson (1985) p. 90 [this is one of the better descriptions of the Redwall section of the Nankoweap Trail]
3 Brian (1992) p. 38
4 Hughes (1978) p. 53
5 Butchart (1976) p. 53 [q.v. Peattie 1958]
6 Annerino (1986) p. 314
7 *Ibid.*, p. 313
8 *Ibid.*, p. 317
9 *Ibid.*, p. 314 [this butte, along with Malgosa crest, are most easily accessed from the river]
10 *Ibid.*, p. 317
11 Hughes (1978) p. 108
12 Annerino (1986) p. 313
13 Hughes (1978) pp. 72, 75-76
14 Annerino (1986) p. 310; Ohlman (N. D.) [personal correspondence files: Interview with Melvin McCormick 9/24/80]
15 Annerino (1986) pp. 313, 315
16 *Ibid.*, p. 316
17 Butchart (1976) p. 57
18 Annerino (1986) pp. 309, 317
19 Schwartz, *et al* (1980)
20 Ohlman (N. D.) [Climbing files; log for 7/9-10/84]
21 Butchart (1976) pp. 57-58; Butchart (1965b) [article on Wotan's Throne and its access routes]
22 Annerino (1986) p. 318 [date is incorrect]
23 Butchart, J. H. personal communication
24 Butchart (1976) p. 58; Butchart (1965)
25 Annerino (1986) p. 314; Ohlman (N. D.) [log for 3/12-20/83, climbing files]
26 Hughes (1978) p. 28; Brian (1992) p. 58
27 Brian (1992) pp. 56, 58; Granger (1960) p. 25

Cheyava Falls in upper Clear Creek.
Photo By: B. Audretch, NPS   Grand Canyon National Park #3999B

46

Main Corridor and Popular Trails

Bright Angel Trail

This is the most popular hiking trail in the Grand Canyon and is usually the first introduction a hiker receives to Grand Canyon. Bright Angel (or B.A.) Trail leaves the South Rim west of Bright Angel Lodge, near Kolb Studio. Originally it was an old Indian trail into the canyon which was improved by Ralph H. Cameron who charged a toll for its use. Cameron was a miner, promoter and sheriff in the area during the 1890's. Along with Pete Berry and his brother Niles, he owned and operated the "Last Chance Mine" below the rim at Grandview. Coconino County operated the trail for a short time before the Park Service took control. Even Santa Fe Railroad fought for control of the trail.[1]

Today, both hikers and mule riders use the trail. Hikers should remember when meeting a mule party they must stand quietly to the side of the trail and allow the train to pass. I have received a few kicks from mules over the years, but luckily none of them were serious. One year the canyon received a heavy snow fall and ice built up on the Coconino sandstone cliff, a Park Service mule train was coming down the frozen switchback and I was making my way up when some very large blocks of ice fell. Several of the trail crew were thrown from their mules. I went to the next switchback to see if anyone was hurt. Luckily, everybody was okay, but shaken up. Mules can be unpredictable animals at times. A wrangler once related a story about a mule that would not let him wear a plastic rain coat. If he put it on the animal would throw him! Generally, though, mule trains will pass hikers without incident. Remember, pay close attention to the wranglers instructions.

Bright Angel Trail follows a faultline with a visible offset of 200 feet. The fault's displacement of the rock strata made a route possible by breaking up the cliffs and forming scree slopes. The faultline runs across the canyon to the North Rim and is the principal reason for the existence of Bright Angel Canyon.[2, 3]

The Kolb brothers established a photographic studio at the trailhead, taking pictures of mule trains for tourists. In the days before the South Rim

Kolb studio 1906; Kolbs on porch. The structure is located at the head of Bright Angel Trail. Grand Canyon National Park #4896

had running water, they used to develop pictures at Indian Garden 3,000 feet below their studio. Legend has it that Emery would take pictures of descending mule trains, run down ahead of them to develop the pictures, then return ahead of the returning train in order to present finished prints to the party![4a, 4b]

The trail begins its first switchback west of Kolb Studio. Not far from the top, hikers encounter an arch blasted out of rock by modern trail builders. Just beyond this first arch are Indian paintings under an overhanging cliff (locally known as "Mallery Grotto"). Some estimate the date of the rock art at 800 years old. About 3/4 of a mile down the trail another arch was blasted from Permian rock.

At 1 1/2 and 3 miles the Park Service has constructed rest houses with drinking fountains which operate during the hot months. Below the three mile rest house there is an impressive series of switchbacks through the Redwall known as "Jacobs Ladder." The Redwall Formation is actually a grey limestone, but staining from iron oxides originating in the layers above tinted the walls red or orangish-red. In this part of Grand Canyon Park the Redwall is about 660 feet thick, but farther west the Redwall forms a wall some 800 feet high. Geologists have dated the Redwall limestone at 500 million years. In contrast, the rim rock, or Kaibab limestone, is 250 million years old and dated to the Permian Era just before the time of the dinosaurs. On the way to Indian Garden a hiker descends eight geologic formations: Kaibab, Toroweap, Coconino, Hermit, Supai, Redwall, Muav and Bright Angel.[5, 6]

Above the Redwall to the northwest stands Battleship and there is a faint trail across Supai ledges to it. A number of people have climbed it from the east side. On top of the summit many names are etched in rock and some of them are quite old.

The distance is a little over four miles to Indian Garden from the South Rim. Water, campsites and picnic tables are available, and cottonwood trees provide shade during the hotter months. There is also a ranger station at Indian Garden. In 1919 when Park Service took control of this area Havasupai Indians were still living at the Garden. A trail leading north out of the Campground will take hikers one and one half miles to Plateau Point; an overlook 1600 feet above the river. Steep walls of the Inner Gorge have been cut over many millions of years by the Colorado River. Plateau Point is an

*The main cables of the Kaibab Suspension Bridge were carried down Kaibab Trail
on the shoulders of Havasupai Indians who were hired by the C.C.C. for the task.*
Photo By: NPS, 1928   Grand Canyon National Park #10,111

50

interesting day hike of about twelve miles round trip from the South Rim with many hikers stopping for lunch here at this overlook above the Granite Gorge. To the west of Plateau Point, growing near a small seep spring at the contact between the Tapeats and older precambrian rock is a ponderosa pine tree. It may be seen from Clear Creek Trail and by the early 1980's had achieved a height of about 40 feet.[7] Three quarters of a mile south of Plateau Point, another spur trail, the Tonto, takes off toward the west. This trail actually crosses Bright Angel and Plateau Point Trails on a nearly 93 mile long journey from Red Canyon to Garnet Canyon. The trail heading west is commonly referred to as "Tonto West." "Tonto East" takes off a short ways north of Indian Garden, before the main B. A. trail drops into the Tapeats narrows of Garden Creek. Signs are posted here warning hikers of some of the dangers involved with hiking the canyon.

Back at Indian Garden, Bright Angel Trail on the east side of the campground leads to the north and begins a drop into the Granite Gorge. There are old Indian ruins in the area. After the trail rounds a bend below the Tapeats formation it descends in a series of switchbacks known as the "Devils Corkscrew." At the base of the Corkscrew the trail drops into Pipe Creek and follows that drainage for about a mile to the river. The River Trail was constructed by the CCC workers in the 1930's and connects the lower ends of Bright Angel and South Kaibab Trails.

It is nearly 8 miles from rim to river via Bright Angel Trail and another 2 miles along the River Trail to the Silver Bridge and Bright Angel Campground.

At the river, signs are posted warning swimmers of dangerous currents and bone chilling water. The River Trail heads upstream to the "Silver Bridge," where hikers can cross, but mules cannot. Mule trains must cross at the Kaibab Suspension Bridge (or Black Bridge), another mile farther upriver. The Silver Bridge was in use by 1970, primarily as a support structure of the new trans-canyon water pipeline which carries water from Roaring Springs, below the North Rim, to Indian Garden, below the South Rim. A pumping station at Indian Garden raises water up to the South Rim and presently is its only source of water. The Kaibab Suspension Bridge was built and rebuilt several times in 1921 and 1928. But the final version was constructed by the N. P. S. for use by mule parties heading for Phantom Ranch.[8, 9, 10]

51

Main Corridor and Popular trails; the most heavily used area at Grand Canyon.

USGS 1962

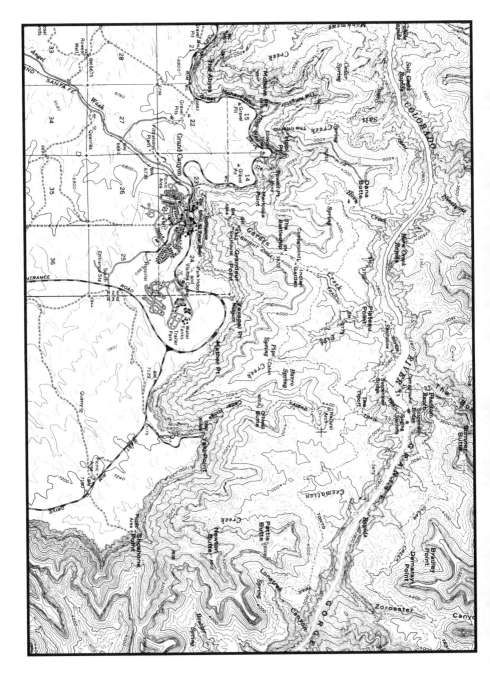

Kaibab Trail

It is a good stiff 20 mile hike from rim to rim in Grand Canyon via the Kaibab Trail. This trail, which runs rim to rim across Grand Canyon was completed in 1928 by the National Park Service. South Kaibab Trail was constructed to avoid Ralph Cameron's toll on Bright Angel. The Park Service took control of the Bright Angel Trail the same year the South Kaibab Trail was opened.[11, 12, 13, 14]

Most hikers take several days to make the hike and there is camping for backpackers at Bright Angel Campground and Cottonwood Campground. Mules and hikers alike use this canyon trail. No water is available on the South Kaibab Trail and hikers should be warned that it is a torturous ascent during the summer. Remember, drink plenty of water and try to avoid hiking at midday during the warmer months. The National Park Service maintains the trail and it is one of the better hiking trails in Grand Canyon. Hikers should remember it takes nearly twice as long to go up as to go down the trail.

South Kaibab Trail leaves the parking lot near Yaki Point and winds down the Permian layers of the Kaibab, Toroweap and Coconino formations. On the north facing slopes, Douglas Fir trees grow near the trailhead. These trees grow in isolated pockets that are shaded during most of the year.

The trail is faint across the red shale of Cedar Ridge before going off the east side of the ridge. On the ridge Park Service has set up a fossil display west of a hitching post.

The trail then stays east of O'Neill Butte descending through red cliffs of Supai formation. Glen Henshaw, Slim Stout and I climbed O'Neill Butte on its west side. It is a very tough technical climb involving use of ropes and climbing hardware. Glen Henshaw is a strong lead climber and we had no serious problems attaining the summit. O'Neill butte was named after an early Grand Canyon pioneer, Buckey O'Neill, who was shot in the throat and killed during the Spanish American War. His name is on the Rough Rider Memorial in Prescott, Arizona.[15] A team of climbers from British Columbia are credited with the first ascent of O'Neill Butte.[16]

The trail has a flat section on top of the Redwall Formation that trail crews for the Park Service call Mormon Flats. Ephedra or "Mormon Tea" grows here. The green sometimes grey bush with jointed stems instead of leaves held medicinal value for early settlers.

54

Kaibab Trail continues off the end of what is known to the mule wranglers as "Skeleton Point." Near a steep drop in the Redwall one can view the Colorado River.

Switchbacks then descend what are known as the "Reds and Whites" winding around to the north of a small unnamed peak which has a small natural arch on its northside. There is an easy climb up the arch from the trail.

A pit toilet is located at the junction of the South Kaibab and Tonto Trails and one can head east or west along the Tonto Platform, the largest bench in this section of Grand Canyon. To the east, is Cremation Canyon. Archaeologists have found "split twig figurines" high up in caves of Cremation Canyon and it is said that the Indians used to cremate bodies of their dead here.[17, 18] To the west is Pipe Creek and beyond Indian Garden and the Bright Angel Trail. There used to be an old wood frame cabin at Pipe Creek, but heavy snows collapsed the room and the N. P. S. deemed it unsafe. Burro Spring should have water.

Beyond the junction the trail drops steeply into the Inner Granite Gorge, where it switchbacks down to the Colorado River. Shortly before the tunnel is reached, a junction to the left leads to Bright Angel Trail by way of the River Trail.

The Kaibab Trail continues thru a tunnel blasted in rock and crosses a suspension bridge built in 1927-28.

There are Indian ruins next to the trail on the north side of the Colorado River as you head for Bright Angel Campground and Phantom Ranch. The Park Service has preserved these ruins with a little enclosure.

Fred Harvey Company maintains a wilderness lodge with meals and rooms to rent at Phantom Ranch and N. P. S. maintains campsites for campers at Bright Angel Campground. Advance reservations are usually required for these. After a long hike on the trail it is nice to either shower or go bathing in the creek. The creek runs clear and cool, and it is such a pleasant relief during the hot summer months. Shade trees and picnic benches line the campground along the creek.

In her book, "Brighty of the Grand Canyon," Marguerite Henry wrote a fictional story about a burro that was found by a prospector running wild along Bright Angel Creek.[19] To the north of Phantom Ranch are some shallow prospects in the canyon near the mouth of Phantom Creek. Beyond Phantom Creek, the canyon opens up and one can see the North Rim. Ribbon Falls is a welcome sight during the summer, where one can stand under the falling water and cool off. A round trip from Bright Angel Campground to Ribbon Falls is approximately 15 miles, and is a nice dayhike.

Almost eight miles north of the Ranch is Cottonwood Camp. Cottonwood is below the Tonto Platform and hikers must continue another six miles and climb 4,000 feet before reaching the end of the trail at the North Rim.

A great buttress below Bright Angel Point is known as "The Devil's Garden." South of the footbridge across Bright Angel Creek there is a good swimming hole that used to have a cable strung across it.

Roaring Springs is an interesting objective for day hikers coming down into the canyon from the North Rim. It is nine miles round trip from Rim to Roaring Springs and back to the Rim. Water is piped to the South Rim from here, flowing by gravity to Indian Garden. At Indian Garden a pump sends the water the rest of the way. Water is also pumped up to the North Rim from Roaring Springs.

About three miles down from the North Rim water is usually available. Farther down in the Supai redrock a trickle of a seep comes down from a cliff above, and I have filled my canteens here.

The passage in the Redwall is one of the most impressive in the canyon and a picture of it ended up on the cover of a 1978 National Geographic Magazine. Trail builders have blasted a trail into the limestone and many places are quite sheer.

Old Bright Angel Trail is a rougher alternative trail to Kaibab Trail and in the spring, crossing the creek can be difficult. The trail through the Redwall is still relatively well defined and there are springs above the Coconino formation in upper Bright Angel Creek. A good solid loop hike for a long day would be to hike down the North Kaibab to below Roaring Springs (cross at the footbridge to the east side of Bright Angel Creek), then go up the Old Bright Angel to the Rim and finish off by following the Ken Patrick Trail back to the North Kaibab Trailhead.

Clear Creek Trail

One third mile north of Phantom Ranch a fork in the trail leads to the east, heading up and over the Tonto Platform into Clear Creek. Mostly waterless, it works its way for over eight miles across a Sonoran Desert landscape of Sage, Mormon Tea, Blackbrush, Acacia and Cacti. The Civilian Conservation Corps built the trail during the 1930's to allow visitors access to Cheyava Falls.[20, 21]

The trail begins a slow ascent of the precambrian rock. Near the top of the Granite Gorge a bench made of stone provides a good rest stop. As the trail rounds the corner below the Tapeats Cliff the Colorado River comes into view. The trail continues below the Tapeats formation until reaching a point just west of Sumner Wash where it climbs atop the Tonto Platform.

Water pockets are in the canyon to the east of Sumner Butte and as Butchart mentions, it is possible to climb up through the Redwall at the head of Sumner Wash.[22] Climbers such as Dave Ganci and John Annerino have used this route to reach Zoroaster Temple. Paul Kelly and I used this slot in the Redwall Cliff to climb Sumner butte; a small triangular shaped buttress, connected to the main Redwall rim by a very impressive knife edge ridge. On the ridge one must go up and over a doorknob shaped rock. Many have climbed through the redrock below Zoroaster finishing up below the peak on its west side. Using ropes to haul equipment is a must and having a strong lead climber in the group helpful. Above the redrock Zoroaster Temple is rated by climbers as a hard 5th class climb involving many pitches. This peak was first climbed by Dave Ganci and Rick Tidrick in 1959.[23] Zoroaster is a character who becomes one of the primary figures in the "Bhagavad-gita" of the Krishna. The Zoroastrian faith still survives today in Persia.[24] Brahma Temple can also be approached from below using the Sumner Wash Redwall route.

Wildlife use Sumner wash too. One day I attempted to climb Sumner Butte by a route below the east side of its saddle. Along the route was lion "scat". Spending most of the day on a failed route I returned to camp. That night a lion came into camp. Startled, the lion cried and ran off into the darkness. Normally I do not camp right on top of limited water sources, allowing wildlife free movement in the area. Perhaps the mountain lion was able to find his way around the camp and go to water 1/4 mile down the drainage.

The trail continues past Sumner wash below Zoroaster Temple and the Redwall, crossing several washes before entering the drainage of Zoroaster Canyon. There is a promontory on the Tonto Plateau between Clear Creek and Zoroaster Canyon and routes exist down both sides of this ridge to the river. From the Colorado River at Clear Creek this becomes a fast way back to the main trail and eventually Bright Angel Canyon. Many of the stronger hikers have used this route.

The trail continues eventually dropping into the Clear Creek drainage. There are good campsites here along side the creek under cottonwoods. During wet weather hikers sometimes use an overhang along the trail high above the creek. I have weathered several storms here and it will keep tent-less campers dry.

Many campers take a day hike to the Colorado River by following the creek downstream. Over the years quite a foot path has developed. Several falls must be bypassed and having good friction soles for a short smear on the water polished granite are helpful. Above the Granite Gorge, east of the mouth of Clear Creek hikers have contrived a route through the Tapeats from the Tonto below Howlands Butte and scrambled down slope to water.

Howlands Butte is climbed via a Redwall route on its southwest ridge. The route is 4th class but a 40 foot section is sort of touch and go without a rope. Howlands Butte was first climbed by Clarence "Doc" Ellis, Borning and Hafterson in 1972.[25] In 1869 the Howland brothers and Dunn left Powell's Colorado River Survey at what is now known as Separation Canyon, climbed to the North Rim and were killed by Indians.[26, 27, 28]

The saddle between Angels Gate and Howlands Butte is endeared with the name "Ball Bearing Hill" by hikers who have climbed through the pass. A scramblers route goes between the peaks, but the southern slope below the saddle has a loose pebble surface. East of Howlands Butte a side canyon drains the Angels Gate/Wotans Throne saddle and ends at a high, but climbable fall below the saddle. I have come down from the saddle and found the rope route to be a good short cut when going between Vishnu Creek and Clear Creek. John Annerino credits the first ascent of Angels Gate to a 1972 technical climb by Dave Ganci and Chuck Graff.[29]

North of Howlands Butte, a notch fault goes up through the Redwall formation in a ravine, south of knoll 6057. Several men have climbed Thor Temple by way of this route, and found the Redwall formation relatively easy. The Supai was a technical climb on its southside, with the most difficult part being a forty foot flake just below the top cliff. The protection in the crack behind the flake was scanty near the top of the pitch. After some time I figured out the right moves, finally making it to the top of the flake. From there a narrow ledge led to a 4th class route to the summit. It was very cloudy and stormy that day and I encountered problems with my orientation. A compass can solve that problem! Al Doty first climbed Thor Temple in 1977.[30] Some climbers have continued to the North Rim from the saddle of Thor via a route near Honan Point, but that route requires a rope. An alternate route through the Redwall exists on the west side of Thor and although exposed does not require a rope.

Upstream from the cottonwood campsite at Clear Creek a trail, not shown on the map, will take hikers up to Cheyava Falls. These falls are impressive in the spring when water cascades down the Redwall. The falls are about seven miles from the camp at the end of Clear Creek Trail. Rangers in 1928 found some ruins near the falls high in a cave.[31] I have never confirmed a route to the North Rim via Clear Creek Canyon but Butchart indicates this is possible.[32, 33] Packard and Walters have climbed out the end of Clear Creek and Bob Dye found a route above the Redwall through the rim cliff somewhere east of Cheyava Falls. Dye's route supposedly used a tall tree to get down the Coconino cliff!

Both Deva and Brahma Temples are relatively easy climbs, but Zoroaster still seems elusive to me (5.8-5.9 via the easiest route). There are two Redwall routes on the Clear Creek side of these temples. Brahma/Deva Canyon goes, as does Deva/Obi Canyon. Both canyons lead mountaineers to red Hermit shale, but the latter is harder.[34] The routes through the Coconino sandstone on both Brahma and Deva are on their west sides. Deva Temple is the easier of the two with a near walk up route over talus with only one cliff in the Toroweap. Brahma Temple has an interesting "V" shape notch in the Coconino sandstone. Climbers start up the northern part of the "V" and then traverse over to the southern part. There are also several Redwall routes on the Bright Angel Canyon side of these three temples, all are south of the Wall Creek drainage. Hattan Butte has been climbed a number of times, but the nameless butte west of the Brahma/Deva saddle may be virgin still. In an interpretation of the Hindu Bhagavad-Gita by A. C. Bhaktivedanta Swami Prabhupada, Brahma is defined as the first created being of the universe; directed by lord Vishnu, he creates all life forms in the universe and rules the mode of passion. Deva is a demigod or godly person. The Oxford Greek-English Lexicon defines Devu as being "flooded with light."[35]

One day Allyn Cureton and I ran down South Kaibab Trail, trotted across Clear Creek Trail, and then went up a canyon to Deva/Brahma saddle. While Allyn climbed Deva, I ate lunch; and when he came down we made a rugged descent into Bright Angel Creek south of Wall Creek, then made our way back up South Kaibab Trail to the rim. Total time elapsed was a little over 20 hours and Allyn Cureton most certainly could have done this in half the time. He holds the record for running rim to rim in Grand Canyon doing it in a little over three hours. I'm sure to be much slower than that speed demon from Williams, Arizona! Allyn said he wants to climb Shiva Temple from the South Rim on a day hike! Whew!

Hermit Trail

Usually after a little experience on Bright Angel and Kaibab Trails, hikers are ready for a more rugged outing on a non-maintained trail. Hermit Trail is one of the more popular non-maintained trails at Grand Canyon.

The trailhead is at the end of West Rim Drive, 1/4 mile past Hermits Rest. Hikers can leave their vehicles overnight at the gravel parking area provided. Originally built by the railroad, and maintained by the Fred Harvey Company for its tourist trade, Hermit Trail was abandoned in 1931 after completion of South Kaibab Trail.[36, 37]

There is some interesting cobblestone work from trail builders in the Coconino sandstone and fossil reptile tracks on some white sandstone slabs nearby.[38] Crossbedding in the standstone show that these cliffs were once sand dunes along an arid coastline. At a junction to the south on the talus below the white rock cliffs, hikers can reach the rim via the Waldron Trail; farther down where red shales meet red sandstones of the Supai formation, the Dripping Springs Trail heads west to a small spring. This spring drips into a basin and it is possible to fill a canteen here (purify before drinking).

Beyond a rest house at Santa Maria Spring, the Hermit Trail continues north, slowly making it's way down through the redrock to a series of switchbacks in the Redwall limestone known as Cathedral Stairs. There are some more steep switchbacks in the grey limestone beneath Cope Butte before the trail reaches its junction with the Tonto Trail on the sloping platform below.

Cope Butte can be climbed from the west via its saddle, and there is a good view of Monument Creek along the route. The way up is "airy" and I would not recommend the climb to a canyon novice.

Beyond the Tonto Trail junction, Hermit Trail doubles back to Hermit Creek. In Hermit Creek are some great swimming holes and an easy foot path leads down to the Colorado River. At the mouth of Hermit large floods have pushed boulders from Hermit Creek into the Colorado River, constricting the flow of the river and thus forming Hermit Rapid. Rafters get quite a roller coaster ride in Hermit Rapid but, swimmers should beware of getting caught in the severe currents. It is also possible to follow the Tonto Trail east around into Monument Creek and follow a constructed trail to the river at Granite Rapids.

One time I was able to hike down Hermit Trail and follow the Tonto Trail east into a small canyon between Monument and Hermit Creeks. It was a rough scramble to the bottom and it was necessary to use a handline to lower my pack; but I was able to reach the river and inflate a small raft, then cross into 94 Mile Canyon. The next day I climbed Tower of Set. It was a technical ascent and I used climbing gear and a rope in two places, spending a good portion of the day on a "self belay." Finally made the summit in the late afternoon and by nightfall was back at my camp in 94 Mile Canyon. I recrossed the river and returned to the South Rim on the third day; totally exhausted, but happy with another Canyon peak under the belt. Butchart mentions a tram survey on the north side of the river here and there was evidence of trail construction atop the Redwall below Tower of Set.[39]

Once in December, I attempted a rugged route between Hermit Creek and Monument Creek below the level of the Tonto Trail. Traversing below the Tapeats Cliff at a difficult spot, the pack rubbed hard against a rock and my sleeping bag popped out, rolled many hundreds of feet down the rocky slope and went into the river. The last I saw it was floating through Hermit

Butchart Hike Map: From east half of Matthes and Evans Topomap. Village and Phantom Ranch, West Rim Trails..

Photo By: M. Quinn, NPS

Grand Canyon National Park #12,786

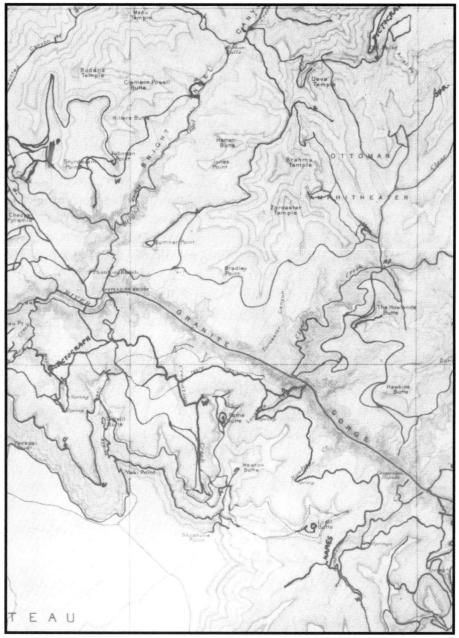

63

Rapid. That night was spent sleeping very cold at Horn Creek. After that incident, the bag always went into my rucksack.

East of Monument Creek, the Tonto Trail continues past Salt and Horn Creeks. There is a route to the river in Horn Creek but one must scramble out of the drainage to the west below the Tapeats formation and then find a slot thru the granite downstream from the mouth of Horn Creek. There is also a small, but permanent seep in the west arm of Horn Creek. I have tried twice to reach the river via Salt Creek, but failed in both attempts. The seep in Salt Creek is bitter, hence perhaps, its name.

Above Salt and Horn Creeks stands Dana Butte with its steep Redwall and nipple shaped summit. Dana Butte still eludes me, although climbers have scaled both it and its northern outlier "Little Dana." Dana Butte was named for James Dwight Dana, Professor of Geology at Yale University.[40] The Bradford Washburn Survey of the 1970's set up a triangulation station atop Dana, using a helicopter to land there. Dana was probably first climbed in 1919 by surveyors working on a cross-canyon tramway.[41]

Still other ways out of Hermit Creek exist. It is very rugged, but you may climb out the head of the drainage to the top of the Redwall. The upper end of the drainage is still relatively pristine. From the top of the Redwall Cliff hikers can traverse back to the Hermit Trail. Hikers can also climb up through the Supai at the head of the canyon and intersect Dripping Springs Trail. This is also known as the "Sewry Route" after an employee at Desert Mountain Sports in Phoenix.[42]

Between Boucher Creek and Hermit Creek, Travertine Canyon provides a not-too-difficult access for hikers wanting to reach the Colorado River. Travertine Canyon is named after deposits of Travertine at and below Tonto Trail level.

1   Hughes (1978) p. 54, 67-68, 88, 90
2   Collier (1980) [general geology]; q. v. Berkowitz (1979); Thayer (1986) p. A7
3   Beus and Morales (1990) [general geology]; q. v.
4a Hughes (1978) p. 72-74; q. v. Verkamp (1993) pp. 26-27 (brief history of Kolbs) Suran (1991) [Excellent overview of Kolbs]
4b Berkowitz (1979) p. 7 [relates story of Kolbs rim to inner gorge antics]
5   Collier (1980)
6   Beus and Morales (1990); q. v. Thayer (1986) (sections A-G)
7   Burak [this information came from Emery Kolb, but River Guides and helicopter and light aircraft pilots have known about this tree for years and often point it out to their guests]
8   Berkowitz (1979) p. 22 [silver bridge]
9   Purvis (1989) [Brief mention of bridges, but long on history of CCC operations in the area during the 1930's]
10 Hughes (1978) p. 88-90 [Kaibab Suspension Bridge]; q. v. Sutphen (1992a) pp. 108-110 [silver bridge]
11 Hughes (1978) pp. 88-90; q. v. Anderson (1992), Sutphen (1991a) and (1992a)
12 Berkowitz (1979) pp. 4-5
13 Verkamp (1993) p. 34, 43
14 Houk (1981)
15 Hughes (1978) pp. 60-62; q. v. Brian (1992) pp. 63-64
16 Annerino (1986) p. 315
17 Brian (1992) p. 63
18 Butchart (1970) p. 17
19 Henry (1991)
20 Hughes (1978) p. 90
21 Purvis (1989) pp. 113-115
22 Butchart (1970) pp. 25-29
23 Annerino (1986) p. 318
24 Brian (1992) p. 62
25 Ohlman [personal climbing files]
26 Hughes (1978) p. 35
27 Brian (1992) p. 127
28 Powell (1961)
29 Annerino (1986) p. 309
30 *Ibid.*, p. 317
31 Butchart (1970) p. 27, 29
32 *Ibid.*, p. 29
33 *Ibid.*, (N. D.)
34 *Ibid.*, (1985) p. 68
35 Brian (1992) pp. 62-63
36 Sutphen (1991a)
37 Thybony (1989) p. 2
38 Butchart (1984) p. 29
39 *Ibid.*, (N. D.)
40 Brian (1992) p. 73
41 Ohlman [personal climbing files]
42 Ohlman (N.D.) [personal climbing files]

General area map, Hermit to Bass.

Courtesy of Arizona Strip District Bureau of Land Management.

66

West to Havasupai

Mooney Falls in Havasupai Canyon.
Photo By: NPS   Grand Canyon National Park #1210

67

Boucher Trail

The Boucher Trail was named after a French speaking prospector Louis Boucher. He was mostly a loner, a hermit.[1] His trail starts on Eremita Mesa across the bay from Hermits Rest. It is one of the more rugged access trails into Grand Canyon. The trail switchbacks down to Dripping Springs and then traverses for about 5 miles along the red Hermit shale. There is a steep grade where the trail goes down thru the Supai formation and when it is wet it can be slippery. The trail then works its way over to the saddle of Whites Butte. Whites Butte was named after one of the earliest prospectors to come to Grand Canyon and start working its cliffs for minerals.[2] Whites Butte is an easy climb and its summit makes a great lunch stop. The peak was climbed prior to 1900.

Quite a bit of trail construction is present in the Redwall formation. Louis had a cabin just south of the trail before the bed of the canyon is reached and it is said he maintained an orchard next to the perennial creek.[3] Beyond a junction with Tonto Trail, the Boucher Trail drops into the bed of a canyon of the same name. A number of mining claims were filed in this area, and an old mine can be seen on the east wall. It is an easy hour or so walk down the creek bed to the river.

Near a junction with Topaz Canyon the Tonto Trail climbs out of the creek and journeys west toward Bass Trail. The next canyon west of Boucher, Slate Canyon, provides the next reasonable access to the river from the Tonto. In Slate Canyon bypass the fall to the east, or down climb directly to the right.

Marsh Butte can be climbed from the Tonto on its east nose and Diana Temple on the west side. Marsh Butte was climbed in 1977 by Mitch McCombs and Pete Baertlein.[4] The route off the rim for Diana Temple begins west of the saddle and just west of Mescalero Point. A climber must then find a break on the northwest end of Diana. Once when leaning back to do a short rappel some zippers gave way on my pack and I lost some canteens into the canyon along this route. Butchart climbed Diana Temple in 1960.[5] Mescalero Point also provides an access route for Vesta Temple.

Going off Jicarilla Point is easier than Mescalero and Pollux Temple was just a scramble. There is a Natural Arch along the western rim of Jicarilla Point and Indian drawings (Petroglyphs) etched in stone along the route. This Jicarilla Point route provides a quick, if not easy access into Slate Canyon. A rope is handy at an 8-10' ledge in the Kaibab, and again in the Coconino where a narrow slot causes problems with lowering of packs. A boulder problem in the Redwall may require using rope for a third and last time before reaching the Tonto Plateau.

An Indian Route off the west end of Walapai Point through the Coconino

Willaim Wallace Bass at the Canyon rim.
Photo By: NPS   Grand Canyon National Park #3635

69

provides access to the Tonto farther west. One must jog south to get through the Supai in the bay, then contour out to the end of LeConte Plateau. A Redwall route is on the west side of the Point and requires a 25 foot rappel. The east side may have a ropeless route.

Sapphire Canyon provides a way to the river from the Tonto Trail. Falls in the bed necessitate climbing high on the west side, then dropping back into the bed, below the falls, then jog upstream at the mouth to reach the Colorado River.

Turquoise also contains a route to the river. Bypass the first fall to the west. There is a tricky scramble to the right of the bed at the mouth. Ruby has a cairned bypass to the right at the fall.

East of Boucher Creek, from the Tonto, hikers can scramble down Travertine Canyon to the river. A good three day hike is to go down the Boucher and camp at the river. Hike the Tonto Trail and camp a second night at Hermit Creek. Then hike out on the third day via the Hermit Trail. Boucher abandoned his trail and moved to Utah in 1912.[6]

Bass Trail

About twenty miles west of Hermits Rest the South Bass trail enters the Canyon and together with North Bass Trail forms one of the few rim to rim trail systems in Grand Canyon. William Wallace Bass came to Grand Canyon in 1884 for his health, but ended up working as a miner, trail guide and hosteler. He married one of his early clients and together they raised a family at his camp on the brink of the Canyon.[7]

Near Bright Angel Trailhead a road heads south and it soon turns to dirt. The road crosses the railroad several times before it leaves the Park. At the Globe Ranch, take the fork to the right. Follow the main trend past Sheep and Homestead Tanks. I usually continue past Lauzon Tank turnoff and enter the Havasupai Reservation before turning north at Pasture Wash. Continue past Pasture Wash Ranger Station (seasonally staffed) out to Bass Camp at the rim. The last five miles can be rough at times.

It is a little over 7 miles rim to river via the South Bass Trail. Even though it is over 100 years old the trail remains in very good condition. The most difficult section to follow is the trail as it traverses the esplanade.

A number of good day hikes can be accomplished from the trailhead.

Chemehuevi Spring, Fossil Mountain, Grand Scenic Divide, Esplanade overlooking Bass Canyon, and Mount Huethawali, among other longer day trips are easily accessed from this trailhead. There is a large overhang below the Esplanade near the head of Bass Canyon and it contains a cooking pot (with the fat still in it), a horse bridle and other equipment. There are also remnants of an earlier trail through the Supai at this place.

Bass climbed Mount Huethawali prior to 1900.[8] Once while climbing Mount Huethawali, I startled a bighorn sheep on the summit. The sheep trail to the top of this summit is not too difficult and apparently the sheep enjoy the view of the Canyon also. Fossil Mountain is an easy scramble along the rim west of Havasupai Point. Another interesting day hike is a traverse east on the Esplanade to a large mesa called Grand Scenic Divide. There are some superb views from the northern end of this long, finger-like mesa. Above Copper Canyon are Darwin Terrace and Huxley Terrace, both excellent day hike destinations.

Bass Trail continues down below the Esplanade via a notch in the redrock east of Mount Huethawali. Bass and other early trail builders placed their trails along faults and other "paths of least resistance." This practice saved on dynamite, but created interesting and long winded trails.

Below the Supai Rim the trail doubles back into the head of the canyon before descending the Redwall. It then sidehills down Bass Canyon. Bass Trail leaves the drainage before dropping to the Colorado River west of Bass Canyon.

From the Tonto you can climb down Serpentine Canyon to the River and routes go to the river in Copper Canyon and across from Hakatai Canyon. A number of old prospects are in the area.

There is an old cable (cut in 1968) that Bass used as an aid to cross the river. Crossing the Colorado River is possible with a small inflatable raft to the North Bass Trail. On the south bank is a boat, the "Ross Wheeler", which was abandoned in 1915.[9] On the northside of the river is Dox Castle, named after the first white woman to cross the Canyon rim to rim.[10] W. W. Bass provided guide service from a trainstop in Ashfork to Kanab, Utah using his inter-canyon trail system.

71

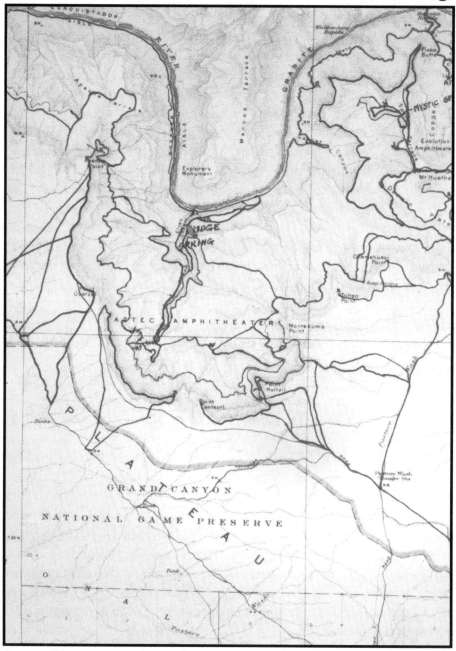

Section of Harvey Butchart's hiking map from Dec. 1975.
Photo By: M. Quinn, NPS

Grand Canyon National Park #12,782

73

Royal Arch Creek

Southeast of Great Thumb Mesa, the Apache Point Trail comes off the rim and works its way east across the Esplanade to Bass Trail. Hikers can occasionally get a glimpse of wild horses on this trail. Mustangs use the trail to go from summer grazing on Coconino Plateau to winter range on the Esplanade. Some of these horses are quite small, having survived for many generations on meager canyon graze.

Apache Point Trail starts down through the Kaibab Limestone near the end of the rim point. Before descending the Coconino Sandstone, the trail circumnavigates a limestone butte sometimes referred to as "Apache Plume." The trail drops sharply through sandstone east of the saddle, but horses seem to make this section okay.

That early Indians used this route is evidenced by a smoke-stained overhang and a mescal pit on Apache Terrace. Not shown on maps, the horse trail continues west across the Esplanade, finally becoming vague near Forster Canyon.

The old, mapped horse trail is faint in places as it crosses the redrock terrace of the Esplanade. It varies in location a little from what is shown on maps, so hikers should follow cairns and horse tracks while navigating this route.

Gary Stiles put a route down to the Esplanade from Point Huitzil. This is a "climbers special" which requires good route finding abilities. Butchart (1984, pp. 36-37) gives a brief description of this route, coming from below. When approaching from above, watch for yellow Toroweap towers which lie north of the route through the Coconino. Other routes in this area which allow one access to the Esplanade can be found off Montezuma Point and Chemehuevi Point.[11]

Buchart was injured once while going down Royal Arch Creek route. He slipped and fell hurting himself seriously enough to be flown out by helicopter. Once atop the Esplanade, there are several routes into Royal Arch Creek through the Supai; the easiest route being a drainage which heads between Points Huitzil and Centeotl. There is a small fall in the lower Supai which can be easily bypassed to either side. The Redwall is straightforward, and one should reach Royal Arch and an impressive Muav fall with little difficulty. Royal Arch, incidentally, is a misnomer as the drainage flows beneath

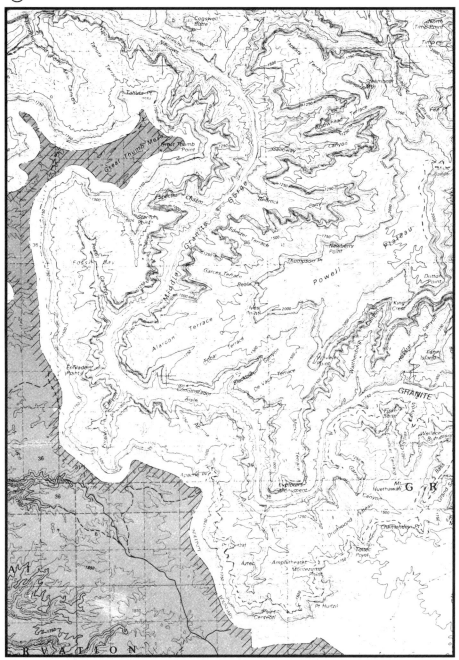

Map of Great Thumb.   Courtesy of Arizona Strip District Bureau of Land Management

75

it, thereby forming a natural bridge, rather than an arch. Waterflow in the Redwall is perennial and can be trusted, even during summer. One cannot reach the river directly via Royal Arch drainage. Instead, backtrack about 3/4 of a mile south of the bridge to a break on the east. Attain the ledge above and follow this north onto the Muav terrace overlooking Elves Chasm. Watch for a huge cylindrical cairn near the corner; remnants of the Matthes-Evans survey. Toward the east end of this terrace, but well before you reach the Toltec Point drainage, look for a pinnacle away from the rim. A 20 foot rappel at this point will get one down onto a travertine shelf, and an easy descent to the river.[12]

You can go down Garnet Canyon (west of the Mount Huethawali saddle) to the top of the Redwall, then traverse at that level around to Fiske Butte. Fiske can also be approached via a chockstone filled ravine at the north end of Spencer Terrace. This was the route chosen by Alan Doty on his first recorded ascent of Fiske Butte in 1974.[13]

140 Mile Canyon

About 35 miles west of Grand Canyon Village an old jeep trail leaves Topocoba Hilltop Road and works its way steadily north out to Great Thumb

Looking for water with binoculars. Photo was taken at the rim of 140 Mile Canyon. Water availability is a definite obstacle to the canyons below Great Thumb Mesa.

Mesa. The jeep trail stretches about 18 miles across Great Thumb, and provides access to Enfilade Point, Fossil Bay, 140 Mile Canyon, Matkatamiba Canyon and to the several routes into Havasu Canyon off Manakacha Point.

From the end of the road above 140 Mile Canyon, an old trail switchbacks down to the Esplanade a distance of about two miles. It is an easy walk from the base of the 140 Mile Canyon Trail out to Olo/140 Mile saddle, from which one can access Key Hole Natural Bridge. It is in this area that the so-called miniature horses can sometimes be seen.[14] The view from on top of Key Hole Natural Bridge is fine, but a view of the bridge is more spectacular from below.

With aid of river rafters I was able to cross the Colorado River from Deer Creek on the north side and climb up into the Muav formation near the base of Key Hole Natural Bridge. Along the way are some Indian ruins upstream from the mouth of 140 Mile Canyon. Bob Euler, Archaeologist at the South Rim for a number of years said there are old Indian sites in the area, as well as mescal pits; especially along the Esplanade. I haven't checked out the southeast arm of 140 Mile, but it would take quite a long rope to rappel through the bridge in the southwest arm.

Colin Fletcher came this way on his 1963 trans-canyon hike from Havasupai to Nankoweap. At 140 Mile Canyon he traversed at the level of the Esplanade until reaching Bass Trail where he dropped down to the Tonto level.[15]

Matkatamiba Canyon

Bob Marley showed me some large potholes full of water near mushroom and hamburger shaped rocks on Chikapanagi Mesa. The water was good and more palatable than some springs and seeps in the area. To the west, Matkatamiba Canyon has a rim to river hikers route. It is a long trek up this canyon and there is a difficult section in the Supai formation where hikers must take off their packs and drag them behind under a narrow steep overhang. There is usually water in Matkatamiba Canyon and Jim Ohlman found some small potholes in the main drainage atop the Redwall. We were able to reach the rim at the 2nd point southeast of Towago Point. Another route through the rim cliffs can be found in the first bay east of Paya Point.

*Bob Marley and Mount Sinyala. Bob has walked from
Diamond Creek to Lee's Ferry.*

A traverse fault line is an aid to hikers going across the Esplanade. The Supai cliffs are broken enough to allow hikers to go across Matkatamiba instead of contouring around on the Esplanade. Some hikers question whether elevation gain and loss is worth the distance saved, but it certainly takes less time to take the shortcut route.

Mount Akaba was first climbed by George Bain of Flagstaff who made a solo ascent in 1980 while on a Colorado River Trip.[16] Others have reached this butte from above via the route east of Paya Point.

Sinyala Canyon

Although there is a spring in Sinyala Canyon on top of the Redwall near its head during times of drought you should question reliability of water here.

The canyon is blocked by a high fall in the Redwall. There is a transverse fault that runs between Sinyala Canyon and 140 Mile Canyon and many hikers claim staying on this fault line is the easiest way across redrock country here. When hiking in Sinyala Canyon I found the amount of elevation loss and gain excessive as compared to a relatively short traverse around the head of the canyon.

It should also be possible to hike around the north and west portions of Great Thumb on top of the Redwall however, this seems to be somewhat contrived and water may become a problem. It is doubtful that a similar route could be followed east and south of Tahuta Terrace. Several hikers have used the Muav ledges to traverse the Canyon to the Middle Granite Gorge.

Southwest of Mulgullo Point are several trails from the rim to the Village of Supai.[17] Carbonate Canyon can also be accessed via the Esplanade and a traverse atop the Redwall over to above Havasu Falls.

Havasupai

Next to Indian Garden and Phantom Ranch, Havasupai is the third most popular destination for hikers in Grand Canyon. There is a reasonable fee for hiking and camping on Havasupai Indian Reservation and this may be handled through their Tourist Office. Advance reservations are a must, however, so write well in advance. There is a store and a snack bar in the village of Supai. All the items sold must be brought in by mule or helicopter as this is one of the more isolated villages in the lower 48 states. The Havasupais restrict travel within Havasupai and into Cataract Canyon, so it is recommended that one contact them at Havasupai Tourist Enterprises, Supai, AZ 86435 (602) 448-2121.

The main attractions are the waterfalls of Cataract Canyon below the village. There is also a campground for hikers and after a long eight mile hike on the Hualapai Trail it is nice to put on a swimsuit and get wet under the waterfalls.

Usual access to Havasupai is the paved road off Old U. S. Route 66 near Peach Springs. There is a parking lot at Hualapai Hilltop along with a hitching post for horses.[18] Horses and hikers both may use this trail. The trail is not very steep and after the upper switchbacks are past, the trail begins to

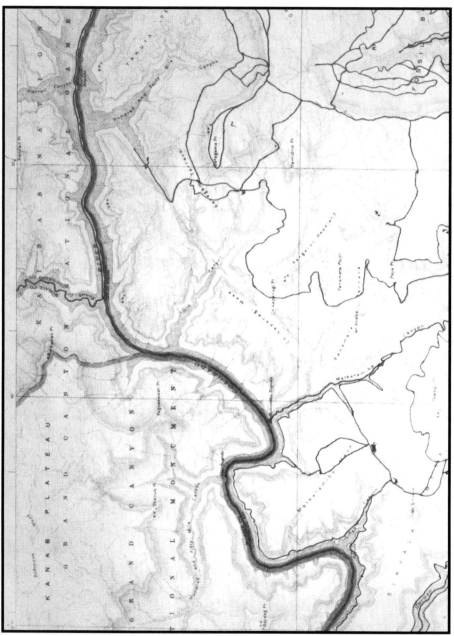

Havasupai area of Butchart's hiking map. J.H. Butchart explored Grand Canyon for over 50 years. Note his route, rim to river just north of Enfilade Point.

Photo By: M. Quinn, March 25, 1994   Grand Canyon National Park #12,783

80

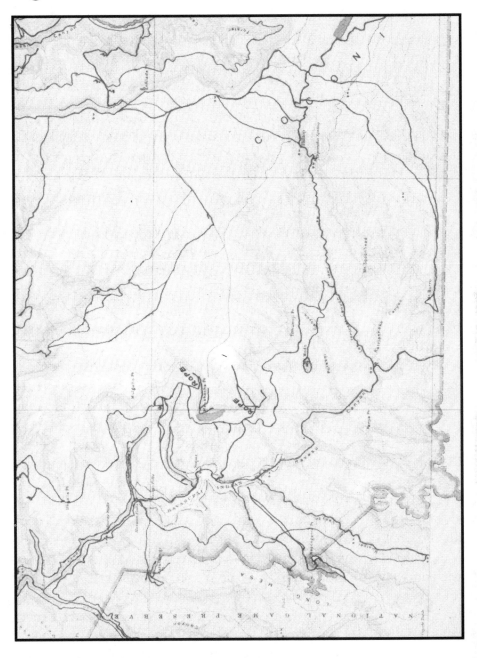

follow the canyon bottom, slowly making its way to the village. There are seep springs on the left before Hualapai Canyon enters Cataract Canyon. In Cataract Canyon, Havasu Springs feed water to the falls farther downstream. At the intersection of the two canyons there are old archeological sites and Indian burial grounds. Please leave all as you find it!

Archaeologists have revealed the area has been occupied since as early as 900 A. D. Population increased steadily until the 1100's at which time a marked decline in numbers was noted, possibly due to intertribal warfare or disease. This decline continued into the 1200's then seemed to level off.[19] Currently the tribe numbers around 400, a few of whom live and work off the reservation in Winslow, Flagstaff, Kingman and elsewhere.[20]

The trail continues down Cataract (Havasu) Canyon and enters the Village of Supai. Standing above the village are the rock pillars of the Wigleeva. These are considered to be the protectors of the tribe and it is said that if they ever fall the village will be no more. The Havasupai acquired their name from the color of the creek water of their canyon home. Havasu means "blue or blue/green water," and pai means "people," thus; "People of the Blue/Green water."[21]

The most impressive falls below the village of Supai are Havasu Falls and Mooney Falls. Havasu Falls is about two miles below the village, and is perhaps the most photogenic waterfall in all of Arizona, with its gracefully scalloped travertine dams and azure tinted pools. Recent flash floods have altered the dams structure somewhat, but it is still the gem of Havasu Canyon. Mooney Falls is about three miles below the village and bears the name of an early miner who lived and died in the canyon. These falls are some two hundred feet high. Here trail builders have cut a steep tunnel into the cliff. To assist with the descent to the base of the falls, a chain was installed and hikers may hold onto it. At the bottom of the fall there is a beautiful pool. Below the pool, water divides into two streams, forming a small island, where Mr. Mooney was buried after suffering a fatal fall while attempting to descend the fall using ropes.[22]

Below Mooney Falls there are a few steep sections of trail and Beaver Falls can be seen at about 3 and 1/2 miles up from the river. While not as spectacular as Havasu or Mooney Falls, Beaver Falls is a favorite day hike destination for river runners. From the campground a day hike to the river

Excavation of ruins at Supai; October, 13, 1938
Photo By: NPS   Grand Canyon National Park #15,578

"Joe"; William Bass' burro on Topocoba Trail. Mail was hauled down to Supai by pack animals on this trail.

Photo By: Peabody 1902
Grand Canyon National Park #828

and back is not too far for the average hiker. Rim to river it is about 33 miles round trip. Jim Ohlman and I made this hike in one day; however we spent 20 hours on the trail. Four days from Rim to River and back would be a more pleasant length of time.

There are other trails into Havasu Canyon. A road crosses the Coconino Plateau from Grand Canyon Village ending at Topocoba Hilltop above Lee Canyon. The Topocoba Hilltop Trail was the old mail route into the village of Supai, and several abandoned vehicles can be seen at the trailhead. One summer the Topocoba Spring went dry and four dead horses were near the top of the trail. This trail is not in as good condition as Hualapai Trail, but there are a few rock cairns to guide hikers along the way.

Jim Ohlman did a technical ascent of Mount Spoonhead on its northeast corner and several people climbed Mount Burro two miles farther south by way of the rim and its saddle. Mount Wodo has a moderately difficult route on its south face, first ascended by Butchart, Ritchey and Price in 1971.[23]

Farther south the next trail access is via Moqui Trail Canyon. The name Hopi is a contraction of "Hopitu," meaning 'peaceful ones,' or "Hopitushinumu," meaning 'peaceful all people.' These people have been popularly known by the name "Moqui," which means 'dead' in their own language, but as a tribal name it is of seemingly alien origin.[24] Bachathavia Spring is a pleasant relief in the summertime. The easiest way to reach this trailhead is by driving south of Pasture Wash. A 4 x 4 may be necessary past Moqui Tank.

Yet other trails and routes exist in upper Cataract Canyon, but many of these are off-limits to non-Indian use.[25]

There is evidence that the plateau above Havasu Canyon was occupied as early at 600 A. D. with peak inhabitation about 900 A. D. Occupation ceased around 1200 A. D., about the same time as the decline of inhabitants within the canyon. Perhaps an outside force drove less protected peoples of the plateau from their homes, or a drought forced them out, yet those in the canyon were protected and had water.[26]

There was a visit from Father Garces in 1776, but after that these people had very few encounters with white folks in the canyon over the next one hundred years.[27] In 1880 the reservation was designated by the U. S. Government as a tract of land about twelve miles long and five miles wide, encompassing the inhabited portion of Havasu Canyon. Two years later it was reduced to an area of 518 acres immediately surrounding the village. In the 1970's the reservation was greatly expanded to its current boundaries (approximately 280,000 acres, both in the canyon and on the rim).[28]

Navajo Falls in Havasupai Canyon.
Photo By: Berezenko, NPS.   Grand Canyon National Park #10,993

1   Hughes (1978) pp. 53-54; Spangler (1986) p. 2, 63; Aitchinson (1985) pp. 123-125; Kelsey (1986) pp. 228-231 [trail data only]; Annerino (1986) pp. 186-189 [good summary]; Butchart (1976) p. 43

2   Brian, (1992) p. 79 [James White was a controversial figure due to his claim to have "run" the Colorado River before Powell]

3   Hughes (1978) p. 54

4   Annerino (1986) p. 314

5   Annerino (1986) p. 311 [rumor has it that Ellsworth Kolb may have preceeded Butchart up Diana, but no solid evidence exists]

6   Hughes (1978) p. 54

7   Hughes (1978) pp. 50-53; Spangler (1986) pp. 107-108; Butchart (1976) pp. 44-47; Annerino (1986) pp. 189-192; James (1900) [James was a friend and confidant of W. W. Bass, and much of his book is devoted to extoling Bass' virtues]; Anderson (1991b) [detailed historical sketch of W. W. Bass]; Babbitt and Thybony (1991) [concise summary of man and trail]

8   Annerino (1986) p. 313; Babbitt and Thybony (1991) pp. 24-25

9   Lavender (1985) pp. 51-54 [Excellent history of G. C. River Runners. Good bibliography]

10   Brian (1992) p. 89 q. v. James (1900)

11   Butchart (1984) p. 36 [GCNP BRO maintains files on trails and routes which may be of value here]

12   Butchart (1976) p. 48

13   Annerino (1986) p. 312

14   Hughes (1978) pp. 93-94

15   Hughes (1978) p. 108 q. v. Fletcher (1967)

16   Annerino (1986) p. 309

17   Butchart (1976) pp. 49-50 q. v. Wampler (1959) [good book covering village area]; q. v. Casanova (1967) [covers some remote trails into Havasu]

18   Annerino (1986) pp. 225-232; Spangler (1986) pp. 46-59

19   Hughes (1978) pp. 11-14 q. v. Hirst (1985) and Illif (1985)

20   Spangler (1986) p. 50

21   Illif (1985); Hirst (1985)

22   Hughes (1978) pp. 47-48

23   Annerino (1986) p. 318

24   Brian (1992) p. 49, 156

25   Butchart (1976) pp. 56-5; Casanova (1967); Aitchinson (1985) pp. 143-144

26   Hughes (1978) pp. 11-14

27   Hughes (1978) p. 14; Spangler (1986) pp. 48-49

28   Hughes (1978) p. 107

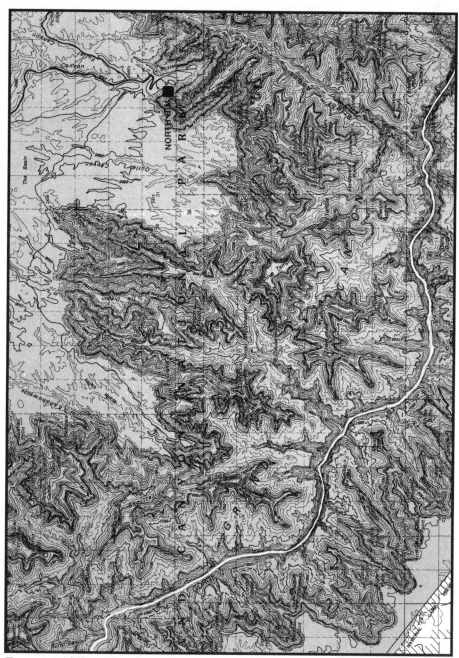

Topo map of Shiva Temple area.

Courtesy of Arizona Strip District Bureau of Land Management

West of Bright Angel Creek

Phantom Creek

Many day hikers venture up Phantom Creek from the Ranch or their campsite at Bright Angel. Narrows of the canyon draw their interest and are surpassed only by those of Zion and Paria. Although not shown on any map, there is quite a foot trail up Phantom Creek to the Tonto Platform. Wear sneakers while hiking up the creek, as it is impossible to make a dry passage and you will get stone bruises on bare feet. Watch for slippery rocks, especially while crossing Bright Angel Creek.

An alternate way into Phantom Creek leaves the northern end of Bright Angel Campground. The trail is steep, but an experienced hiker will not find it difficult. The plateau above Bright Angel Creek is known locally as "Utah Flats." From here it is possible for a hiker to traverse the slopes north of Cheops Pyramid to below the Isis/Cheops saddle. Scrambling east down a ravine here will bring one to the Tapeats formation, a short traverse will lead one to the creek and upper Phantom Creek Valley. Hikers can also pass westward over the Cheops/Isis saddle into the drainages of 91 Mile and Trinity Creeks.

Unlike Bright Angel Campground where Fremont Cottonwood trees abound, Narrowleaf Cottonwood trees grow along the course of upper Phantom Creek. A walk into the upper valley is pleasant indeed.

Yet another way into Phantom Creek Valley is from the North Kaibab Trail along an old cattle trail. This trail leaves Bright Angel Canyon east of Hillers Butte, and contours around the base of Johnson Point. Two springs are passed enroute, one south of Johnson Point and another southwest of Sturdevant Point. A descent to the valley is just beyond the canyon east of Schellbach Butte.

At least four routes come into Phantom Canyon off the North Rim. The easiest of these leaves the rim west of Tiyo Point and descends to the Shiva/Rim saddle. There are several routes through the Supai, but all involve using a large bay east of Shiva Temple. The Redwall break is north of Isis/Shiva saddle, on the west side of Phantom Canyon. Note: this route is much easier

89

going up than coming down. A second route involves leaving the rim on the west side of the point overlooking the Colonade. Once below the Kaibab and Toroweap, one traverses over to the Colonade saddle and drops through the Supai on the east side of that saddle, heading along a path that will place one atop the Redwall at the upper end of Haunted Canyon. A rope is necessary to lower packs at either of two places in the Redwall, but day hikers have done the more western route without a rope. A third route descends the bay due west of Widforss Point and will get one down to the Redwall breaks mentioned above. Although possible to do this route without a rope, I'd take along a 150' rope to rappel past a bad place in the Coconino. I can't recommend this access for overnight use as it is too dangerous to contend with packs on the rappel and subsequent traverse. Climbers have also come down into Outlet Canyon, and succeeded in rappelling through the Redwall. At least one hiker has fallen here, so expect no easy route up.

Hikers have climbed to the top of Johnson Point on a day hike from Bright Angel Campground. The way up is via a talus slope through Muav formation on the west side of Johnson Point and after a short traverse the Redwall is climbed up the ridge point. There are some good views of Bright Angel Creek from on top of Johnson Point. Both Hillers and Clement Powell Buttes have been climbed via a Supai route east of their saddle. Clement Powell Butte bears the name of John Wesley Powell's brother, while Hillers was one of the great photographers of the American west. Both men were on Powell's second expedition.[1]

To climb Schellbach Butte use a canyon between it and Sturdevant Point (locally called "Sturdevant Canyon"). Park rangers Tom Davison and Mark Sinclair said it was possible for a climber to descend north of the saddle through the Redwall along a small fault ravine. Climbers use a rope in this ravine and it is much more difficult than the Sturdevant Canyon. A chockstone fall must be down climbed and the moves are very strenuous. I ended up doing a full length body jam to pass below the fall on the right. The route is an interesting, but rough way to descend into Haunted Canyon.

Cheops, Isis, Shiva, Manu and the Colonade I have climbed. Manu Temple was done by way of a route west of Widforss Point. It is an easy climb up ledges and chimneys. Harvey Butchart and Alan Doty pioneered a way off the rim north of the Colonade and using this route I soloed the Colonade on its north face; a moderately easy fourth class route.[2] Hauling packs with a handline is a wise idea and those sqeamish about heights should not venture on this Canyon peak at all. On the summit is a register in a small plastic bottle that contains the name of a Flagstaff climber. He had carried Harvey Butchart's summit log to the peak in 1993, although Alan Doty had the first recorded ascent in 1970.[3] On both sides below the saddle a scree slope is an easy scramble to the top of the Redwall formation.

Buddha Temple is accessed using either the Widforss Point route or the Colonade route from above, or the "Sturdevant Canyon" route from below. Above the Schellbach saddle one can get through the upper Supai in the bay north of the temple. Buddha is a moderate 5th class climb via a ravine on its southeast corner (eastside). It was first climbed however, by Grubbs, Brown and Parker in 1972 via a different route on the west side of its northeast ridge.[4]

Trinity

It is a six to eight hour hike from Bright Angel Campground to Trinity. Water is available down a rough trail in 91 Mile Canyon, but a hiker must go all the way to the river to get it. "Utah Flats" has some small rock overhangs which provide shelter during storms, and the trail leading up from the north end of Bright angel Campground is not too difficult for an experienced hiker. The fastest way to reach the pot hole water in Trinity Creek is to head along the northeast side Cheops Pyramid. Cross the Isis/Cheops saddle then swing around south of Isis Temple atop the Shinumo Quartzite. Cheops Pyramid can be climbed from the saddle, while the southern outlier (sometimes called "Agassiz Spire") must be approached from the south. The route up from the Isis/Cheops saddle is unique in that it passes over a natural bridge of limestone. Merrell Clubb is credited with first ascents of both the Pyramid and its outlier.[5]

Pothole water is available in Trinity, and overhangs in the Tapeats formation make for good camping. There is an alternate route onto the plateau above 91 Mile Canyon from Bright Angel. One follows the Colorado River downstream from the Bright Angel Creek about 1/2 mile then ascends through a break in rim cliffs of the inner gorge. I found this route more difficult than the one that leaves the north end of Bright Angel Campground.

Isis, Shiva and Osiris along with Tower of Set can be climbed from Trinity Creek. Shiva Temple is by far the easiest to climb and is accessed via a Redwall break on the southwest side of the Shiva/Isis Saddle. Here, a great block of limestone has fallen and hikers must pass beneath it. A hand line to move packs can be helpful. The Supai break is to the north of the Shiva/Isis saddle in a bay due east of Shiva. There are at least three routes up Shiva from the top of the Esplanade which encircles it. The fastest route goes up a ramp and chimney system on the east side of the northeast arete. This route was used by members of the 1937 Shiva Temple expedition.[6] An easier, albeit longer route is via a deer trail in the largest bay on the southwest side of the butte. A third route goes up on the north side of the ridge heading west toward Claude Birdseye Point. The last route is rough and is really only useful for those wishing to climb Shiva and Birdseye on the same trip.

I climbed Shiva Temple when about a foot of snow was on the ground and had no problems with water, but did have to fight hypothermia. The weather socked in bad and it was necessary to use a compass to find a way across the top of the Temple. I followed my footprints in the snow back to my camp atop the Supai. One December night a bull elk bugeled while on the deer trail south of Shiva Temple. The next day I followed his tracks to the Birdseye/Osiris saddle. A number of years ago a small herd migrated from southern Utah to the Kaibab Plateau, but it is amazing they would want to winter in the Shiva area!

Al Doty told me of his climb of Isis Temple and I decided to repeat it. Ended up using a climbing rope and equipment on the peak and it is a satisfying climb, especially solo. Initially one must traverse the top of the Redwall below Isis and start up the Supai formation west of the Cheops promontory. Coming to the top cliff in the red rock traverse back around to the promontory above the Isis/Shiva saddle and find a technical route a short distance around to the south. Between the two summits the Coconino break is on the east side of Isis below the saddle. Follow the ridgeline north from the saddle. The lower, southern summit can be climbed separately on its south end.

Technically, during good weather, Osiris Temple is not as severe a climb as Isis. One December I was able to climb up most of the Supai formation near the Osiris/Ra saddle. Then it was possible to traverse north, below the Esplanade and climb the final supai cliff northeast of the summit. There are several ways to scramble through the Coconino sandstone on the southwest side. Weatherwise, I was climbing in a sleet storm that did not clear off until 3 o'clock in the afternoon. Making the summit late in the day, darkness fell during the return series of rappels through the Supai cliffs north of the peak. The storm made me hypothermic and when clouds cleared the temperature dropped sharply. In the darkness my flashlight dropped, going out some forty feet below me. Not having made it past the cliffs I was unable to get back to my sleeping bag that night. It was a very cold December night as the South Rim recorded a temperature of 0 degrees. Unable to continue in darkness for fear of running out of rope the option for a very cold night seemed logical. Without a stove or a sleeping bag and only wearing a wool sweater, the situation was serious. To stay alive that night I burned some of my climbing sling along with every dead bush within reach. NPS frowns on open fires, especially those using native vegetation as fuel, but as the saying goes, "desperate times call for desperate measures!" It was one of the most miserable nights I have ever spent and I learned a great deal from it. Incidentally, Osiris was first climbed by Donald Davis in September of 1966 using a Redwall route to the north of the Ra/Osiris saddle.[7] When I climbed the peak I found his summit register.

Tower of Set was a technical climb for me, yet I've heard of others doing it "free". I climbed Set on its north side from Horus/Set saddle following what I believe to be Bruce Grubbs and Jim Haggart's 1977 route.[8] Horus Temple has eluded me, but there is a moderate 5th class route somewhere on its southeastern promontory.[9]

There is no route through the Redwall into Trinity Creek from Birdseye/Osiris saddle, but climbers have discovered a route through the Redwall into Crystal/Dragon Creek west of Osiris. Next to following the Tonto, the easiest way into Dragon Creek from Trinity would be by way of the Shiva/Rim saddle. This route is easy enough for an intermediate bushwhacker.

Below Tower of Set one can reach the river from the Tonto immediately upstream of 94 Mile and it takes most of one day to walk from Trinity Creek to 94 Mile Creek. There is no good water other than the Colorado River at 94 Mile. From the mouth of 94 Mile, hikers must head north up the drainage for about one mile to a route up to the Tonto or stay below the Tapeats in the Granite Gorge. George Steck details an alternate route directly up to the Tonto from the mouth of 94 in his book, Grand Canyon Loop Hikes I.[10]

Butchart line map.
Photo By: M. Quinn, NPS

Grand Canyon National Park #12,780

In Egyptian mythology, Set killed Osiris, and Horus avenged Osiris by killing Set. Isis was Osiris' wife and mother to Horus. Set was the nasty uncle to Horus.[11]

Crystal Creek

The easiest route into Crystal Creek is by way of the Shiva Saddle. Park on Tiyo Point Road and hike west to the ridge that leads south to Shiva Saddle. A scramble off the North Rim is not too difficult for intermediate bushwhackers and there is now a visible trail in the Coconino. This rough trail makes a rapid descent to the saddle below Shiva Temple, where water-filled pot holes remain for a week or more after rainstorms. The route continues west off the saddle into the short easy arm of Dragon Creek. Boulder hopping seems to be the rule in this side canyon.

Downstream from where this canyon intersects Dragon Creek, water first appears in the drainage bottom. Near Dragon Spring a fall in the Tapeats must be bypassed. The bypass is steep and I slipped not once, but twice; sitting on cactus both times. Hindu Amphitheater is unique in that it has no constructed trails.

Following the canyon bottom of Dragon and Crystal Creeks to the river is certainly no harder than Clear Creek. In 1966 a great flood pushed huge boulders into the Colorado River, transforming a rather meek riffle into one of the most impressive rapids in Grand Canyon. The rapid is quite a maelstrom of white water, and roar of its rushing water can be heard at quite a distance. High releases of water from Glen Canyon Dam during the summer of 1983 were responsible for many capsized river rafts, and one man succumbed to hypothermia after flipping his craft in Crystal Creek Rapid.[12]

Just a short distance up Crystal Creek to the east George Steck found a route to the Tonto Plateau from the inner gorge. Steck then contoured east along the Tonto, dropping into 94 Mile Creek by two different routes. The easier of the two lies much nearer the head of the canyon while another goes off the end of the Tonto point.[13]

Farther north from Crystal Rapids there are rim to river routes down both arms of Dragon Creek. I have also climbed up through the Redwall from the drainage bottom between the two arms of Dragon.

You can climb Little Dragon, Dragon and Dragon Head from the North Rim but I encountered thick brush on the ridgetops. All these are easy 3rd class scrambles.

Jim Ohlman showed me a route off the west side of Grama Point and we climbed Confucius Temple by a steep sandstone ramp on the south face. The ramp contains a large number of fossil amphibian tracks preserved in Coconino Sandstone. Jim went ahead that day and climbed Mencius Temple on its southwest side. In the mid 1980's a mid-air collision near Mencius Temple between an airplane and a helicopter claimed many lives. Much of the wreckage ended up on the Tonto below the peak. Bodies were flown out of the canyon by helicopter, and little evidence remains of the crash site.

Harvey Butchart, Tony Williams and a number of other canyon enthusiasts have hiked over the Flint/Tuna saddle. The Tuna side is the easiest end of the trek. George Steck includes a good write-up of a loop hike utilizing this saddle in his book, G. C. Loop Hikes I (pp. 49-67).

Ruins east below Point Sublime indicate an old Indian trail off the rim here. In 1980 old corn cobs were evident under an overhang so the Indians that lived here must have farmed either the rim or a canyon delta in this area.

With the Colorado River on the rise, Harry McDonald left the 1889-90 Stanton Expedition and climbed out to the North Rim via Crystal Creek. He "post holed" through deep snow for several days before reaching a dwelling at V. T. Park. McDonald later prospected throughout eastern Grand Canyon.[14]

North Bass Trail

North Bass Trailhead is most easily reached via a dirt road that leaves the highway near Kaibab Lodge.[15] Rains can be torrential on the North Rim and Swamp Ridge received its name with a certain degree of accuracy. After storms I have seen logs floating on the road with water running brisk and several feet deep.

Bass Trail above Muav Saddle was improved by the C. C. C. during the 1930's and is fairly well defined as it makes its way through upper Permian strata. There is a small cabin on the saddle that I have used for refuge during thunderstorms.[16] During the summer of 1981 the spring southeast of Muav Saddle was dry, although this spring generally flows yearlong.

Horse hanging from cable car, Bass Ferry.
Photo By: NPS, 1917

Grand Canyon National Park #6000

North of Muav Saddle an old trail comes down to the Esplanade west of Crazy Jug Spring. This trail is not shown on current topo maps, but some old versions of the Forest Service map showed a trail. Forest Service personnel have also scrambled down routes to the Esplanade via Timp and Fence Points, and Parissawampitts Canyon. I do not know if Powell Spring is reliable. During the summer of 1981, I had problems locating any water at all on the brushy Esplanade.

From Muav Saddle another trail continues up and across Powell Plateau to Dutton Canyon. A mile walk beyond the end of the trail brings one to Dutton Point. Dutton Point is an exceptional scenic vista, from which the mountains south of Ashfork and Seligman can be viewed.

Harvey Butchart has climbed Steamboat Mountain north of Powell Plateau however, the route below the Plateau is very brushy across the Esplanade.[17] Jim Ohlman suggested a route that would avoid the brush leaving the rim of Powell Plateau on the west side of its northernmost point. Other routes to the Esplanade exist along the narrow, west-facing side of Powell.

North Bass Trail is washed out and brushy below Muav Saddle, but there are numerous rock cairns set up in the Supai to provide direction. Below the Supai the trail starts out clear, but becomes increasingly vague as one nears the Redwall descent. If you start to see panoramic views of the canyon while traversing along the top of the Redwall, you have gone too far. Double back to find where the trail makes its descent. Once on the trail through the Redwall it is easy to reach the bed of White Creek. White Creek has perennial flow, and was named after a prospector who built the upper portion of North Bass Trail to access his copper mines on the Coconino below Swamp Point.[18]

The trail again becomes vague as it heads down the creek below the Redwall. It seem easiest to stay in the creek bottom down to the Tonto. The trail avoids a fall in the Tapeats cliff by leaving the drainage to the west and dropping back down some 2-1/2 miles later, near the junction of White and Shinumo Creeks. An alternate route is to follow a trail of use into Redwall Canyon, and descend that canyon back into White Creek below the fall.

Shinumo usually has perennial flow, but in 1982 it was dry above Flint Creek junction. This is one of the more pristine areas of Grand Canyon and willow trees add particular charm to the canyon.

Section of Harvey Butchart's hiking map. Powell Plateau/Thunder River areas.
Note National Forest Boundary which in the 1970's was relocated to the rim.
Photo By: M. Quinn, March 25, 1994, NPS   Grand Canyon National Park #12,781

100

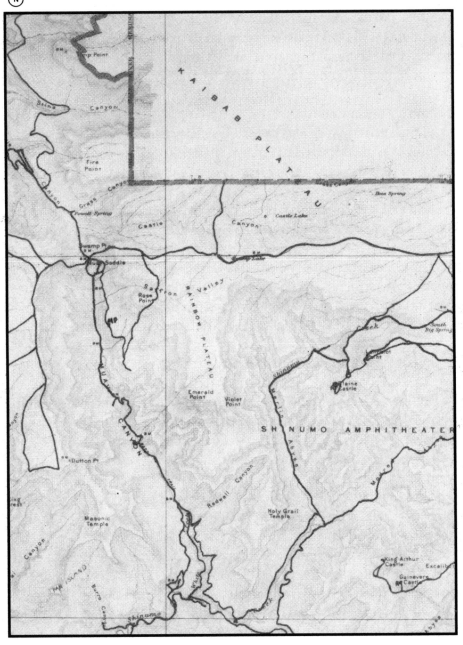

Many of the drainages below the Muav formation have water in them. Gawain Abyss has tall walls and is dry for the most part. Jim Ohlman and I checked this canyon out and were surprised at the discrepancy in the topographical map. Contour lines of the 1:62,500 scale map do not show the severity of the walls. We came to the conclusion there was no way for hikers to climb out of Gawain Abyss.[19]

Dedicated canyon hikers have succeeded in climbing out of Flint Creek, reaching the rim northwest of Point Sublime. Ropes are necessary to haul packs, and those with a sensitivity to heights should not attempt a Redwall climb here.

Elaine Castle is an easy climb via a route off the south end of Lancelot Point. One summer's day Ohlman and I climbed Elaine, and noted a ruin near the summit that Butchart mentions.[19b] It is possible to descend the Supai and the Redwall on both sides of the Elaine Castle saddle. The northern route is slightly more difficult, and hikers should lower their pack using a handline. One can also descend into Shinumo from South Big Spring but there are some cliffs along the way that must be bypassed, and brush is bad.

Leaving the Swamp Ridge Road at Swamp Lake, Ohlman and I climbed the small unnamed peak X7125 in the northern section of Shinumo Amphitheater. This "Merlin Castle" was first climbed by Alan Doty, and requires use of a rope. Jim succeeded in jamming knots of climbing sling in a vertical crack of rock for some forty feet, although very small stoppers or wired hexes would have worked better if we'd had them. Excalibur and Holy Grail have both been climbed, but they are not easy. Excalibur, along with King Arthur and Guinevere Castles are accessed via a ravine off the rim point, south of Galahad Point. Excalibur requires technical equipment, but the two castles are easily climbed on their south sides. Holy Grail is easier than Excalibur, but the approach route off Violet Point is tedious.

Jim Ohlman and I climbed Masonic Temple on a day hike by coming off the rim on North Bass, traversing the top of the Redwall then climbing up through the Supai formation east of Dutton Point. Some route finding and a little climbing are involved at Masonic Temple saddle, but the view from the summit is superb. We then traversed below King Crest, passing a ruin along the way, and climbed up to Powell Plateau via Dutton Canyon. The route through the Coconino is south of the head of Dutton Canyon. We returned to

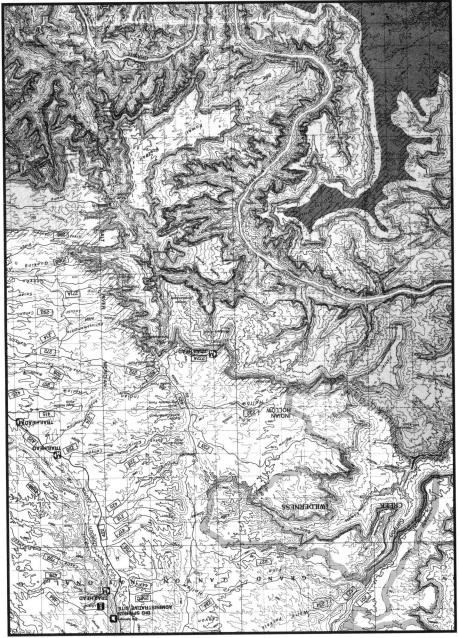

Powell Plateau area.

Map courtesy of Arizona Strip District Bureau of Land Management

103

the rim by way of the Powell Plateau Trail, reaching our vehicle just past sundown. Al Doty is credited with first recorded ascents of both Masonic Temple and King Crest, although he found ruins near the summit of King Crest.[20]

Bob Packard, Ken Walters and Donald Davis have traversed much of the Esplanade below Powell Plateau, and George Steck and others have circumnavigated the Plateau along the river and Tonto using the North Bass and Tapeats Creeks for entrance and exit.[21] While there are a number of rim to Esplanade routes off Powell Plateau which allow access to Steamboat Mountain, Alarcon and Marcos Terraces, and Masonic Temple, there are no known ropeless routes through the Redwall anywhere around Powell Plateau except via Saddle Canyon and the North Bass Trail. One near-ropeless route exists east of Explorer's Monument, but it has limited value for non-climbers; one can easily rappel down it, but only strong climbers can go up.

Portions of a constructed trail still exist in Burro Canyon, where W. W. Bass accessed Tonto Plateau west of Shinumo Creek. He used this trail to reach his asbestos mines in Hakatai Canyon and an extension of this trail reaches the river just downstream of the mouth of Hakatai.[22]

Walthenberg Canyon has some interesting narrows below the Tonto, but several long bypasses are required to reach its mouth. One can next reach the river in the ravine east of Explorer's Monument.[22b]

Although vague in places, there is a fairly continuous trail system from Shinumo Creek to near Blacktail Canyon along the Tonto Platform.

George Steck describes a harrowing experience he and his companions had at the mouth of Saddle Canyon in his second book, Loop Hikes II.[23] They were one day into a long trip around Powell Plateau when their camp was inundated by a flash flood. No one was lost or seriously inconvenienced, but many articles of clothing, etc. were sacrificed to the river Gods that day. Saddle Canyon provides a moderately easy route into Tapeats Creek when it is dry, with only a bypass or two in the Supai and some stagnant pothole pools to contend with in the Redwall.[24] It is not, however, a good place to be during flash flood season!

Explorer's Monument, Fan Island and Dox Castle are all moderate 5th class climbs.[25] Dox has a clever route on its south side, toward the middle; Fan can be climbed on either the west face, or via a chimney-like route near its southwest corner; Explorer's Monument has an intricate route utilizing the Redwall and Muav ravine to the east, and has also been approached from above via Powell Plateau and Marcos Terrace. A slot on its northeast end gets one up the Supai caprock.

Thunder River Trail

The Thunder River Trail was constructed in 1876 and rebuilt by the U. S. Forest Service in the 1920's as a stock trail.[26] This trail can be approached either from Indian Hollow, or via a spur called the Bill Hall Trail which leaves the rim on the east side of Monument Point.[27]

Below the rim seasonal pothole water is available, but hikers must search hard for it on the Esplanade. Slim Stout and I climbed Bridgers Knoll below Monument Point and found it to be a non-technical peak. A long day hike would consist of going down Thunder River Trail to the Falls and back to the rim. The main attraction of this area of Grand Canyon are the falls. Flow from several openings in the cliff is substantial, and cavers wearing wetsuits have explored several thousand feet of subterranean passages behind the falls. Water flows down steep cliffs which are decorated with Monkey Flowers, Maidenhair Ferns and other riparian flora. Backpackers can hike from the falls to the Colorado River via Tapeats Creek, encountering only a few obstacles along the way. In wet weather, however, Tapeats Creek may be running high enough to be unfordable (check with NPS Backcountry Reservations Office before hiking).

East of Thunder River, one can hike up Tapeats Creek and exit to the rim via Saddle Canyon or Crazy Jug Canyon. Saddle Canyon is a direct route, but the Redwall in Crazy Jug should be climbed to the west, about 1/2 mile up from the junction. The Supai break is west and north of where you top out on the Redwall, and the rim break is on the west side of Crazy Jug Point.

Along the Colorado River, Stone and Galloway Canyons are good day hike destinations from a camp at Tapeats Rapids. From the confluence with the Colorado River it is possible to hike downstream along a rugged sheep trail to a point above Deer Creek Falls. However, it is much easier to access Deer Creek via the trail leading west in Surprise Valley below Cogswell Butte.

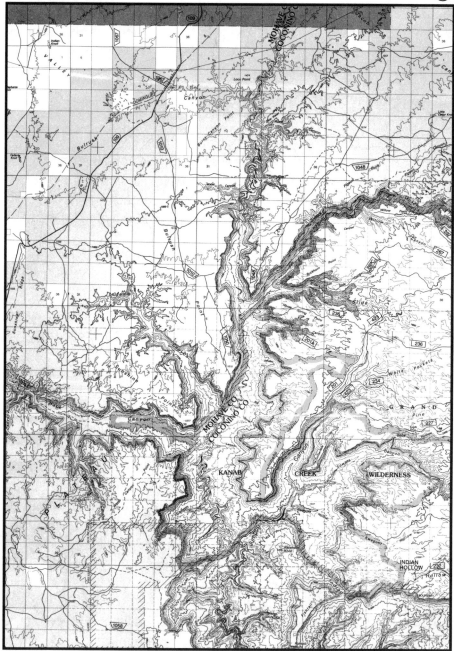

Topo map of upper Kanab Creek.

Courtesy of Arizona Strip District Bureau of Land Management

106

Cogswell is an easy scramble to the top via the northern slope. From the summit are fine views of the Colorado River.

A great slump of limestone has fallen away forming Surprise Valley and some geologists have theorized it was the result of a giant cavern collapsing or slumping toward the void caused by the river removing support along the south.

Deer Creek Trail is not hard to follow and there is evidence of early man in this canyon. River runners like to use water from the fall to fill their water jugs, although it should be treated as some folks have taken ill from drinking unpurified water from this creek.[28] Standing under the cold shower is nice in the summer time, but one must brace against the hard downpour.

The angled canyon between Fishtail Canyon and Deer Creek is sometimes called "Cranberry Canyon," owing to a Redwall route discovered there one Thanksgiving by David Mortenson. George Steck and Harvey Butchart describe this route in detail in their guides.[29]

A constructed trail comes down into the east arm of Fishtail Canyon from the Esplanade, and Harvey reports a spring in the lowest Supai there. By staying atop the Esplanade, one can traverse west from Thunder River Trail and cross over the saddle east of Fishtail Mesa.[30] Fishtail can be climbed from this saddle, and splendid views can be had from its overlooks. Indian Hollow is directly accessible from this saddle, and Steck describes a scrambler's route up to the rim at the head of this canyon.[31]

Over the years many hikers have made their way down to Kanab Creek and the footpath is easy to follow. On a week long outing it is possible to hike the Sowats/Thunder River Loop.[32]

Kanab Creek

Kanab is a Paiute Indian word meaning willow. There are quite a number of jeep trails in this area of western Grand Canyon that provide access to the mega canyon. The Kanab Creek Wilderness is a fine place to hike on trips as short as a day hike to those exceeding several weeks.

It took me seven days to hike from Fredonia down Kanab Creek Gorge to the Colorado River. Another two days were required to hike from the river and climb out to the rim of Kanab Plateau via Chamberlain Canyon. The drainage bottom goes dry for a long stretch below Fredonia and hikers must rely on a few springs and occasional pothole water.

I was able to fill my canteen at Clear Water Springs, located in Kanab Creek a short distance above Rock Canyon. Cowboys have built a trail down the west side of the gorge here and it was fun to sit in the shade of the spring and watch them herd cattle. It should be possible for hikers to

The Redwall narrows of Jumpup Canyon.

scramble out east to the top of Clear Water Point from the spring. Downstream from Clear Water Spring, Kanab drainage goes dry again.

There are room outlines at the mouth of Rock Canyon, evidence of early presence of man. Below Rock Canyon it seems easiest to stay on the Toroweap ledge for a couple of miles to avoid brush in the drainage bottom of Kanab.

An impressive butte stands across from the mouth of Gunsight Canyon. Once again there was evidence of cowboys who have built a fence on the saddle of this unnamed butte. Hikers can traverse the ledge above the creek on a well defined trail, go over the saddle, then descend to the dry bottom of Kanab downstream from the butte.

Twice now I've found water at the junction of Snake Gulch with Kanab Creek. Near the junction there is a metal shed and cowboys have built a rock wall; an old washed out jeep trail also comes down Snake Gulch. This road was closed after the creation of the Wilderness Area. Old timers still refer to Snake Gulch as Shinumo Wash, not to be confused with the areas of North Bass or Marble Canyon.

There are many ways into the upper reaches of Kanab Creek. Slide Canyon provides a trail from the rim to a spring, but I found the spring choked with brush. Both Burnt and Grama Canyons can be hiked without much difficulty. Gunsight Point has a route to the east (Swapp Trail #50) which provides a way from the rim to the canyon bottom in Snake Gulch.[33]

Butchart mentions in his book "Grand Canyon Treks II" that main access to Kanab Creek is by dirt road into Hack Canyon. Just around the corner from where the road stops, the canyon opens up into a cut through the Esplanade. Willow Spring is reliable. Behind the mine near a parking area there is a vague trail to the rim used by deer and sheep. During the 1970's and 1980's uranium ore was removed from the Hack Canyon Mine and hauled to processing plants in southern Utah. One can find bits of black igneous rock in the drainage that has come down off Kanab Plateau. To the north of Willow Spring a break in the rim leads up to Sunshine Point and a road on top provides vehicular access. Hikers have also come down Water Canyon from Kanab Plateau into Hack Canyon.

Directly across from Hack Canyon a deer trail leads up Lawson Canyon to the rim and Jumpup Point. This makes an interesting day hike from Willow

Spring and the view from Jumpup Point on National Forest land is breathtaking.

Below Jumpup Point, Ranger Trail winds along the Esplanade, essentially connecting Snake Gulch with Jumpup Canyon.[34] This trail is faster than busting brush in the creek bottom. It is possible for strong walkers to hike from Cove Canyon to Jumpup Canyon in one day. The Forest Service has marked the trail fairly well and it is one of the more pleasurable hikes in Kanab Canyon. There is pothole water below Jumpup Point and Indian paintings on a wall underneath an overhang. The overhang is smoke stained and there is evidence that mescal was roasted here. Ranger Trail crosses Jumpup Canyon continuing across Esplanade to Sowats Canyon. Butchart reported a pack trail going down to a spring east of Sowats Point.[35]

A Forest Service road comes down Jumpup Canyon to the top of the Toroweap. There are several springs in the upper canyon and good overhangs for camping near the lower spring. Butchart mentions that lower Jumpup Canyon is level and easy down to the actual Jumpup.[36] A makeshift ladder helps hikers past a fall below Lower Jumpup Spring and it took me awhile to figure out where the route was. Below the fall and ladder the bed is easy. Sowats usually has a small stream flowing into Jumpup Canyon. Below Sowats the bed is dry again as one walks through the Redwall narrows of Jumpup. Hikers have also gone up to the rim via Kwagunt Hollow.

Along with water, Butchart noted tire tracks near the junction of Kanab and Jumpup Canyons.[37] In 1994 the junction of Kanab and Jumpup was dry, but down Kanab several miles water appeared in the drainage. West of Racetrack Knoll, Packard and Walters have climbed down an unnamed canyon leading to Kanab Creek.

George Steck outlined a trip up Indian Hollow in his book "Grand Canyon Loop Hikes I." He encountered a fall with a plunge pool and on one trip had to swim ten times to bring all his gear across to complete the route. The fall can be bypassed on the right during cold weather when swimming is undesirable.[38]

Both Fishtail Mesa and Racetrack Knoll have been climbed. Racetrack is the easier of the two; Fishtail Mesa has several routes on its east end and northern side. In 1980 Forest Service employees told me about remnants of a trail on the north side of Fishtail Mesa saddle. Once, while flying over the canyon with the National Guard, I spotted a very large pothole of water on the Esplanade southwest of Fishtail Mesa. The pothole is located high above the junction of Kanab Creek and the Colorado River.

The small unnamed canyon south of Chamberlain Canyon has an old horse trail from Kanab Creek up to the Esplanade. Hikers can also climb out Chamberlain to the Esplanade. A fall in the Supai is bypassed on the left. Above the Esplanade there is a very difficult route out the head of Chamberlain Canyon. The scree slope up to the Coconino and Toroweap is steep. A large unstable flake is perched on a cliff as an obstacle along the route and there are many difficulties for a solo hiker trying to haul his rucksack on a 50 foot handline. I needed to crawl under a narrow overhang with 70 feet of exposure near the top of the Toroweap formation. From there, the drainage in the Kaibab was easy. A route to the rim in Chamberlain Canyon is easier farther east, via a ravine coming in from the south. It is possible to hike the Esplanade between Chamberlain and Burnt Canyons using a vague trail on the Esplanade.

Below the junction with Jumpup, the Kanab drainage is not too difficult and only a few places boulders have choked the creek making hiking miserable. A few miles south of the Jumpup junction a spring appears in the canyon bottom and water runs the rest of the way to the Colorado River. I made a camp and started the next morning with a light rucksack. It was a long day hike from the spring down to the river and back again, but the walk was well worth the effort. Kanab Creek is one of the more pristine areas of Grand Canyon. Fish are only a short distance from where the spring starts and I found that very surprising.

Some hikers have come down the large canyon between 150 Mile and Chamberlain, but you should understand this route is difficult. "Scotty's Hollow" route is described by Steck and Butchart.[39] Deep pools of water present an obstacle in the side canyon leading south to the red rock rim. It would be interesting to use this route then hike around the Esplanade into 150 Mile Canyon.

Powell's second Colorado River survey left the river at Kanab Creek in 1872. Dellenbaugh wrote: "Sunday was spent resting here, and Thompson took observations for time. On Monday morning we expected to pack up again and proceed down the gorge, but Powell, instead of directing this course, announced that he had decided to end the river work at this point on account of the extreme high water, which would render impassable the rapid where the Howlands and Dunn had left. In addition, word was brought that the Shewits were in a state of war and had resolved to ambush us as we came down, a plot that had been revealed by a friendly member of the tribe to Jacob Hamblin."[40]

View upstream of the Colorado River at Kanab Creek. Powell's second Colorado River Survey left Grand Canyon at this point.

1   Brian (1992) p. 68; Annerino (1986) pp. 311, 313
2   Butchart (1984) p. 25
3   Annerino (1986) p. 311
4   *Ibid.*, p. 310
5   Annerino (1986) p. 310; q. v. James (1900) [uses the name "Agassiz Spire" p. 134]
6   Hughes (1978) p. 93; Annerino (1986) pp. 89-90; Brian (1992) p. 74
7   Annerino (1986) p. 315
8   Annerino (1987) p. 317
9   Ohlman (N. D.) [climbing files: Letters from Ken Walters and transcribed log from Bruce Grubbs]
10 Steck (1989) pp. 39-40 [pp. 33-47 outline many of the routes in Phantom, Canyon Trinity Creek and along the Tonto between Trinity and Crystal]
11 Brian (1992) p. 75; Granger (1960)
12 Steck (1989) pp. 38-39; Butchart (1976) p. 60; Lavender (1985) pp. 53, 119
13 Steck (1989) p. 38
14 Butchart (1976) p. 59; Brian (1992) p. 80; Lavender (1985) pp. 29-30
15 Steck (1989) p. 70 [Road Log to Swamp Point]; Kelsey (1986) p. 198; Babbitt and Thybony (1991) p. 30 [Road Log]
16 Babbitt and Thybony (1991) p. 34
17 Annerino (1986) p. 316; Butchart (N. D.) [q. v. log for 10/17/64]
18 Brian (1992) p. 90; Granger (1960) p. 25
19 Hughes, and others
19b Butchart (1976) p. 62
20 Annerino (1986) pp 314-315
21 Steck (1989) pp. 69-87 [circumnavigation of Powell below the Redwall]
22 Steck (1989) pp. 85-86; Hughes (1978) p. 52; Butchart (1976) p. 46
22b Steck (1989) p. 84
23 Steck (1993) pp. 223-228
24 Steck (1989) pp. 76-77
25 Ohlman (N. D.) [climbing files; also logs for 3/15-24/80 and 10/24-26/80]
26 Anderson (1991a); Annerino (1986) p. 258; Hughes (1978) p. 90
27 Butchart (1976) pp. 63-64; Annerino (1986) pp. 258-261; Aitchinson (1985) p. 133; Kelsey (1986) pp. 200-201; Brian (1993) p. 103; Steck (1989) pp. 88-89 [Road Log to Indian Hollow]
28 Steck (1989) p. 95
29 Steck (1989) pp. 94-95; Butchart (1984) p. 46
30 Butchart (1984) p. 45
31 Steck (1989) pp. 107-108
32 Steck (1989) pp. 88-108; Steck (1993) pp. 229-233
33 Kaibab National Forest (N. D.) pp. 14-19 [Brief description and maps of Swapp Trail #50, Slide Spring Trail #11, Slide Canyon Trail #58, Snake Gulch-Kanab Creek Trail #59, Ranger Trail #41, and Jumpup-Sowats Point Trail #8 access roads shown also]
34 Kaibab National Forest (N. D.) pp. 16-17 [Ranger Trail #41]
35 Kaibab National Forest (N. D.) pp. 18-19 [Jumpup-Sowats Point Trail #8]
36 Butchart (1975) p. 28
37 Butchart (1975) p. 28
38 Steck (1989) pp. 106-107
39 Butchart (1984) pp. 46-47; Steck (1989) p. 105
40 Dellenbaugh (1902) p. 341

View west from Toroweap; Ranger John Riffey in foreground. To the right, a lava flow from Vulcans Throne provides access to the river via Lava Falls Trail. Eons ago lava flows formed natural dams in this area of Grand Canyon. Cutting action by the Colorado River eroded these igneous dikes. Many geologists attribute the travertine deposits in Havasu Canyon to the large lakes which formed after these periodic flows. Other dams existed downstream, one near the mouth of Spencer Canyon.

Photo By: S. Leding, 1952, NPS   Grand Canyon National Park #2368

Tuweep to Kelly Point

Tuweep

Many postcards of Grand Canyon show Toroweap Overlook, a view point which towers some 3,000 feet above the Colorado River. Here a dirt road goes right to the rim of the gorge where one can view Lava Falls Rapid.

Of course hikers always want to go down the steep, loose, Lava Falls Trail. The trailhead lies west of Vulcans Throne, a small cinder cone located on the brink of the gorge. Extreme care should be exercised in descending this 1 1/2 mile trail, as the lava is crumbly.[1] At the base of the trail is the largest rapid in Grand Canyon, and a ride through it is exhilarating. Hikers have also climbed out of Prospect Canyon across the Colorado River from Vulcans Throne. Harvey Butchart found a way up the middle of the wash out Prospect, but it involved some very steep scrambling.[2] Climbing "The Anvil" is possible, but the need of a boat arises because the rock is located in the middle of the river.

For many years Ranger John Riffey was stationed here at Tuweep Ranger Station, flying in and out of the area with his airplane "Pogo." He used an airfield in Toroweap Valley which he made himself. When Riffey died he was buried near the Ranger Station that he had manned for some 40 years.[3]

Behind the Ranger Station it's possible to climb to the top of Toroweap Point on the Kanab Plateau. Broad Canyon also will take hikers to the top of the Kanab Plateau without difficulty.

South of the Ranger Station a road leads toward The Cove at the base of the Uinkaret Mountains. The cinder cone of Mount Emma reaches up to an elevation of 7698 feet. This peak was named after John Wesley Powell's wife.[4] Loose cinder is steep near the top, but the view from the summit is worth the struggle.

Looking several miles north from Mount Emma one may note a trail leading to the summit of Mount Trumbull. The trailhead starts across the road from the Forest Ranger Station at Mount Trumbull. It takes several switchbacks to reach the summit. The mountain stands at over 8,000 feet and was named

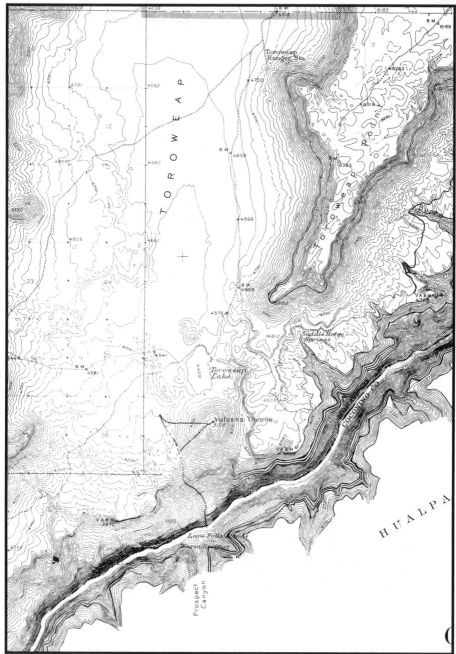

Lava Falls area.   1944 USGS Topo Map

116

Tuckup Canyon and Kanab Plateau. Main access roads are #1058 and #1057. The author found driving at night between 150 Mile Canyon and #109 road very confusing. During wet weather four wheel drive is advisable.

Courtesy of Arizona Strip District Bureau of Land Management

117

after Senator Trumbull who helped J. W. Powell win financial support from congress for his survey in the Canyon.[5] Mount Trumbull Wilderness Area is an interesting place to spend a day. Early Mormon pioneers logged this area of the Arizona Strip, using timber for the construction of the Temple in St. George, Utah. Logs were hauled by animal teams across the Arizona Strip and taken into Utah via the "Old Slide Road."

West of Mount Emma a jeep trail winds its way down Whitmore Wash to end at the Whitmore trailhead. Whitmore Canyon was named after an early Mormon settler.[6] Great lava flows from the Uinkaret Mountains have poured down into Whitmore Canyon. It is possible to walk the Esplanade from Tuweep to Whitmore Trail along an old road. One year the road to Whitmore trail was so rough that it took 3 1/2 hours to cover 23 miles with a four wheel drive.

Farther east, Steck showed me a rappel route to the bottom of 150 Mile Canyon where he has walked above the river along Muav ledges to Kanab Creek. Steck credits Robert Benson Eschka with pioneering the river route between Kanab and Tuckup.[7] Steck also forged a route along the river downstream beyond Tuckup Canyon; however, this route is slower and more tedious than Tuckup Trail on the Esplanade.

Sue Smith found a box of explosives in 150 Mile Canyon dating back to the 1950's. There are seep springs in 150 Mile Canyon and water is also available on the Esplanade below S. B. Point above the mouth of Tuckup Canyon. S. B. Point was named after a cattle brand used on Kanab Plateau.[8] Tuckup Trail received its name from the old Tucket Mining District.[9]

Many tributaries on the west side of Tuckup Canyon have springs in them. Sue Smith found a reliable spring in Cottonwood Canyon and there is an old mining prospect is nearby. The Esplanade below Big Point also has a large seasonal pot hole. Some 65 miles in length, Tuckup Trail may require six or more days to hike between 150 Mile and Tuweep. You can hike downstream from 150 Mile Canyon along the Muav ledges to Tuckup Canyon and then climb out the main drainage during the course of a week. George Steck showed me the northern most fork of Tuckup Canyon and it is an easy scramble to the rim. There are also trails down from the rim to Schmutz Spring (named after a rancher) and down Willow Canyon to the Esplanade. Near Schmutz Spring are some interesting paintings under an overhanging cliff. They seem to depict blue coat "Long Knives."

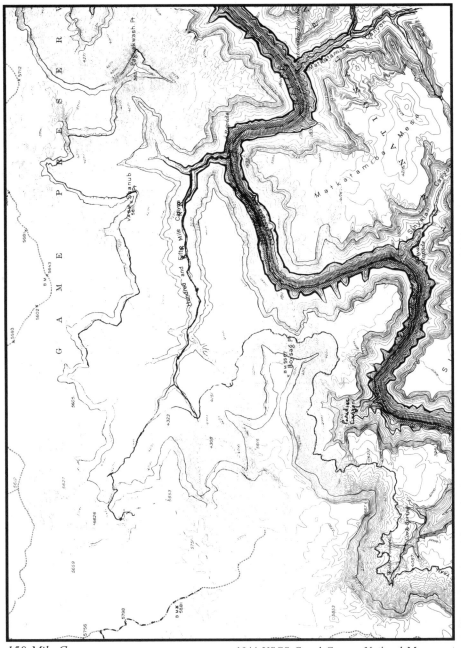

150 Mile Canyon area.   1944 USGS Grand Canyon National Monument

119

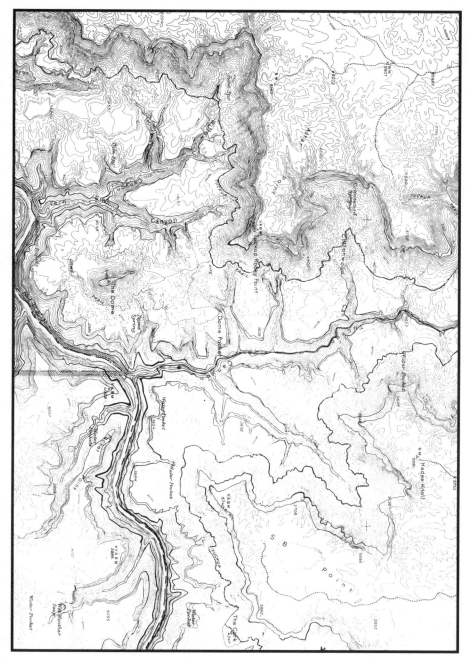

Tuckup Canyon.

USGS 1944 Grand Canyon National Monument

120

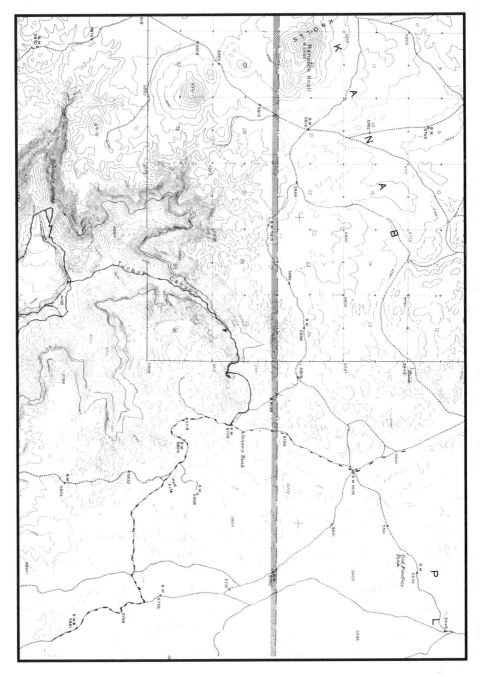

Paguekwash Point may be climbed from the rim saddle or from below, east of the saddle. Paguekwash is a Paiute word meaning fishtail.[10] Climbing the Cork is an easy scramble on black igneous rock. The 1944 edition of the Grand Canyon National Monument Map shows Cork Spring to the east of the peak and several parties have found the spring to be reliable. Technical climbers have climbed the Dome and it is certainly one of the hardest peaks to climb in Grand Canyon. Across the river, Flat Iron Butte is an easy climb via a chimney route on the east side and seasonal pot hole water is available on the Esplanade. Vulcans Throne located in Tuweep Valley is an easy cinder-cone climb and affords some rather nice views of Western Grand Canyon.

The map shows a spring located near Toroweap overlook and after rainstorms there is pot hole water on the Esplanade. France has a large, open city park in Paris called the "Esplanade" and perhaps this is where the term comes from.[11]

Rim between Bundyville and Snap Point

Settlement of this remote area on the Arizona Strip began around 1916 through an application for 640 acres of land. By the 1930's nearly 250 people were living in the area. Homesteaders raised livestock, but subsistence and cash crops were wheat, corn, beans and squash.[12]

It is about 60 miles from St. George, Utah to the crossroads of Bundyville on the Arizona Strip. The present school was built in 1922 and was in use until 1966. This structure was built from wood that was cut on Mount Trumbull and Mount Logan then brought down the "Old Slide Road" by horse drawn wagon. The road was so steep that workers had to tie down the wagon wheels and skid them down the incline.[13]

The road leading south, from the school house, leads to a ranch in Whitmore Canyon some 15 miles distant. Another fork, to the west, will take people down a rough road in Parashant Canyon to the Esplanade. The east fork goes to Nixon Spring and Mount Trumbull.

In Main Street Valley, north of the crossroads of Bundyville, a road leads west across the rim country above Western Grand Canyon. At the road fork stands Diamond Butte. Referring to naming of the peak during the Powell Survey, Dellenbaugh wrote: "It had no name in our language, and I did not

122

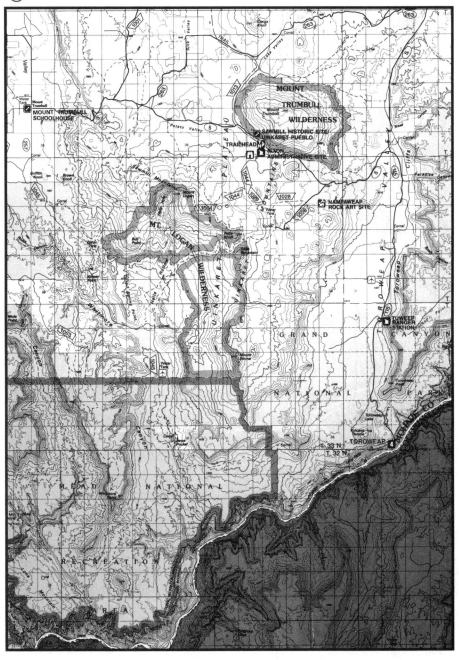

Tuweep area.   Courtesy of Arizona Strip District Bureau of Land Management

Schoolhouse at the crossroads of Bundyville; most easily accessed via Main Street Valley Road, south of St. George, Utah.

know the native ones, so, remembering that at the foot of one I had found some ant-hills covered with beautiful diamond-like quartz crystals, I called it Diamond Butte..."[14]

The road passes the head of Andrus Canyon and continues on toward Poverty Mountain. North of Poverty Mountain the road enters into McDonald Flat at the extreme upper end of the Parashant drainage.

Before Oak Grove Ranch is reached there is a turnoff to Mount Dellenbaugh. Park Service maintains a seasonal fire guard station here, and an old jeep trail leads up toward Mount Dellenbaugh. Another road heads south from the Ranger Station, toward Kelly Point overlook above Grand Canyon. Beyond Green Spring the road becomes very rough with tank trap size rocks in it. Off to the west both Dinner Pockets and Ambush Pockets are deep, reliable pools of water. From the road, Price Point makes an interesting objective for a day hike and the view of Western Grand Canyon is superb. A route to the river starts down from the rim southwest of the point. I used this route to traverse rim to rim via 205 Mile Canyon. Farther south, the head of 209 Mile Canyon offers another break in the rim rock that will allow hikers down to the Esplanade, but this road is rough and four wheel drive is required. Back at the Oak Grove Fork, a road heads south then west passing the heads of Twin Springs Canyon and Twin Creek Canyon. The road then heads south for Twin Point. Less than a mile south of the Oak Grove a road leads west to Snap Canyon and a small cabin on the Sanup Plateau. It is a distance of over 90 miles of dirt road from St. George, Utah to a seep spring in Snap Canyon. The road continues across the Esplanade to Grand Gulch Mine. Glen Henshaw and Slim Stout experienced difficulty when attempting to go down the Grand Wash Cliffs by four wheel drive because roads were severely washed out.

Whitmore Canyon

If you are to head south from the crossroads of Bundyville, it is 15 miles down to Bar 10 Ranch in Whitmore Canyon. There I met Berdon Heaton, a cowboy for the last thirty years in the area, and he told me about hiking opportunities at Whitmore.

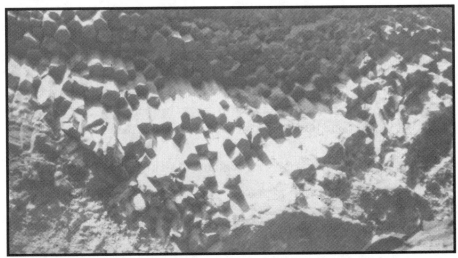

"Devils Postpole;" along the Whitmore Trail. Basaltic rock here displays polygonal shapes. Some geologists theorize magma contacting oil and aluminates caused this unusual formation.

125

A trail up Mount Emma takes off from behind the ranch house and heads up the slope, but it soon becomes vague and hikers must climb for nearly 4,000 feet without a trail. Above the white cliffs the slope becomes forested with cedar and pinion and a view from the summit is well worth the effort.

South of Bar 10 Ranch a fork in the road leads up southeast to Paws Pocket, but Berdon Heaton said water there was not reliable. A rough, washed out jeep trail winds around the Esplanade to just below The Cove, stopping short of a corral. To the east is the road to the Lava Falls Trail (now, impassable over its entire length).

Back on the Whitmore road, another fork, this time leading towards small cinder cone, will take hikers to Cane Spring Trailhead. The trail starts on the west side of the hill, southwest of the cinder cone. This trail shows a lot of construction work and it passes a cliff on the left with inscriptions. Some of them are quite old, dating perhaps early as the late 1840's during Mormon settlement. Cane Spring was improved with some storage tanks within the last 20 years.

Back on the main Whitmore road heading south, one climbs up over a ridge and begins a steep descent to Whitmore Trail. Slim Stout and I used a four wheel drive for this section of the road in 1981. Whitmore Trail drops 1,000 feet through a series of switchbacks to the Colorado River. The trail is quite scenic and it passes a 'Devils Postpile' formation of basaltic rock overhead. The trail ends at a sand beach upstream from Whitmore Rapids.

In going up the main bed of Whitmore Canyon from the river, hikers are stopped by a high cliff. A trail bypasses the fall to the west, close to the Colorado River and immediately downstream from the mouth of Whitmore Canyon. Berdon said that before the road was put in, the original Whitmore Trail came down from Cane Spring.

For hikers wanting to go from Whitmore to Tuweep via the Esplanade, a Redwall ridge northeast of the trailhead offers an interesting alternative to traversing the basaltic flows. Upstream from Whitmore Trail a steep canyon comes down steeply to the river offering climbers a route to the Esplanade. Farther upstream a route along the river is blocked by a high cliff before Lava Falls is reached.

At Whitmore Trailhead there is an old cowboy line shack and a horse trail leads to the north, crossing Whitmore Canyon above the fall. After crossing, the trail heads west toward Cane Spring.

Unusual rock outcrop below Whitmore Point.

Above Cane Spring the jeep trail continues across the Esplanade be-yond a severely washed out section and heads west between two unnamed peaks. Both of these peaks can be climbed without technical climbing gear. There are some good views from the jeep trail of Tommy Mountain and the Hualapai Reservation. I followed this road on foot for a full day from Cane Spring, heading north around the bend towards Frog Spring. I was unable to find a route through the Esplanade to the spring, but discovered a pot hole of water at the canyon east of where the road ends. Some Supai overhangs were suitable for camping that night. The next morning was spent climbing out the ridge leading to Whitmore Point. This ridge has its ups and downs. At one place I had to climb down partway on the west side of the ridge and a large red cliff in the Hermit needed to be bypassed to the east, along a bench similar to that of the Supai formation in the eastern part of the park. The white rock is relatively straight forward and it was necessary to take off my pack in only two places because of narrow cracks along the route. A scree slope immediately east of the point provides a route from the Esplanade above Cane Spring to the rim. It is a short walk from Whitmore Point to a road that heads north to Bundyville.

127

Parashant

From the crossroads of Bundyville a jeep trail makes its way into Parashant Canyon and the Esplanade red rock. Near the bend in the road to the west, there is a small canyon with a seep spring called Cup. The road continues, crosses the main Parashant drainage, and then passes Copper Mountain Mine. This mine is fun to poke around in and Jim Ohlman found some good fluorite mineral samples.

The road continues west across the Esplanade to Andrus Canyon. Andrus was a Mormon militia officer during early settlement of Southern Utah and the Arizona Strip.[15] I have climbed Andrus Point from the east. Northwest of

Upper end of Parashant Canyon; note road. Cup seep is located in the small canyon to the left.

Andrus Point it is possible to climb up to the rim from the Esplanade; note: Coconino sandstone is just a few feet thick. It is also possible to hike up Andrus Canyon from the Esplanade to a small ranch on the rim. At one time a road may have come down Andrus Canyon to the Esplanade, but it is no longer there. To the east a large basaltic flow covers the rim. A good portion of Shivwits Plateau is blanketed by black lava rock.

Beyond Andrus Canyon the road gets rough. A tell tale oil stain from a fractured transfer case was evidence someone ran into a good size rock on the jeep trail. It is possible to hike up to Shivwits rim south of Dansill Canyon. A vague trail traverses a long bench of lava rock before it reaches the rim northeast of Yellow John Mountain. Cattlemen have installed some unusual one-way gates along the way. I have climbed down from the Esplanade to Dripping Spring and Lost Spring, but these are probably not reliable water sources. Muddy Spring may not be reliable, but a cistern called "Midas" is farther south on the Esplanade. A good day hike from the cistern is out to Mollies Nipple and back along a jeep trail. The road passes several mescal pits and a smoke stained overhang. Climbers can make an ascent of Mollies Nipple by a route above the saddle, but it is rather "airy." A route northwest of Mollies Nipple will take a hiker to the top of Shivwits Plateau. Packard and Walters located a route below Mollies Nipple down to the river at the Parashant delta. Of course it is also possible to continue southwest on the Esplanade to a basalt slide below Price Point.

Both Andrus and Parashant Canyons will take hikers to the river without much difficulty, but a solo may want to use a handline to lower his pack. Parashant Canyon has some impressive narrows as it passes through Temple Butte limestone. Cedar Spring that Butchart mentions was just a muddy seep in 1982.[16] One may continue down to the Colorado River with no significant obstructions beyond the junction of Parashant and Andrus. The entire length of Parashant Canyon is dry except during wet weather. I saw mescal pits at the mouth of Parashant Canyon and it is possible to hike both up and down river from the delta. It is about 8 miles down the right bank of the Colorado River to Spring Canyon along an old burro trail that follows the river. Ohlman and I were unable to find the Indian paintings that Butchart describes as located three miles downstream from the mouth of Parashant Canyon.[17] Immediately downstream of Spring Canyon is a rough game trail going up limestone that will take one to the Esplanade and the Price Point route. If there ever was a constructed trail here it has been obliterated by time and elements.

Upstream from Parashant brush becomes thick; Ohlman and I struggled a great deal to reach the base of Billingsley's Frog Spring route. A rope is handy for raising packs on this route. A fault line fracture in the strata allows one to climb all the way up a canyon southeast of Lone Mountain. Reliability

Kelly Point.   Courtesy of Arizona Strip District Bureau of Land Management

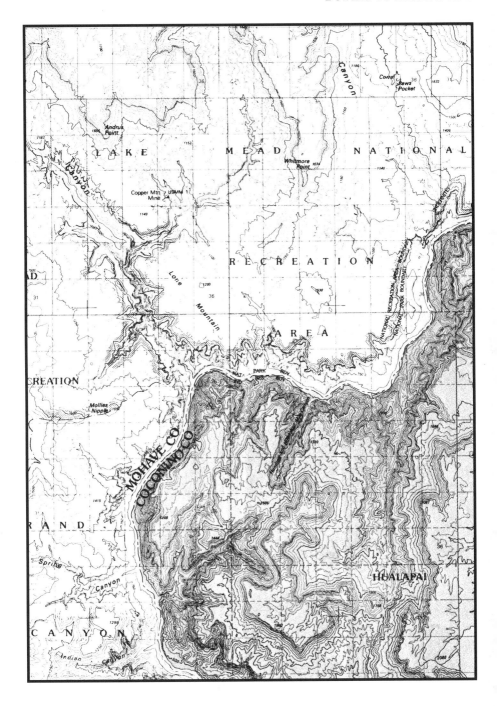

of springs around Lone Mountain I am not sure of, but a hiker can take the terrace traverse over to investigate them. We were able to continue north on the fault line and proceed down a trail dropping back into Parashant Canyon near a rock slide that knocked the trail out. Jim found large pot holes of water in a canyon leading up to Copper Mountain Mine. Glen Henshaw later found a way to climb up to the Copper Mountain Mine, thus avoiding boulder-hopping in upper Parashant Canyon.

Whitmore Point is an easy scramble from below and it is possible to walk to the Esplanade over to jeep trails in the Whitmore drainage. You can climb Whitmore Point from the ridge that divides Parashant from Cane Spring. Southeast of Whitmore Point the map shows the location of a spring named "Cane."

Certainly more ways from the River to the Esplanade exist between Whitmore Trail and Billingsleys route up to Frog Spring. Butchart made the difficult traverse between Parashant and Whitmore along the river cliffs. Where these cliffs meet the river upstream from Parashant, hikers may continue upstream along a bench of Muav.[18]

Parashant is derived from two Paiute words for water and elk.[19]

Spring Canyon

There are many breaks in the rim southwest of Mollies Nipple that provide a route from Shivwits Plateau to the Esplanade, north of Spring Canyon.

From the river you may hike up Spring Canyon for nearly a mile before being stopped by a fall. Near the mouth there is a Spring.

Immediately down river from Spring Canyon a route goes to the Esplanade via the ridge between Spring Canyon and Indian Canyon. There are some room outlines on the Esplanade saddle. The route continues to the rim south of Price Point, where Butchart reported some large water pockets.[20]

209 Mile Canyon

When hiking on the Sanup Plateau with Jorgen Visbak he told me of his hike down 209 Mile Canyon. There are several routes off the rim near Price Point and also near the head of 209 Mile Canyon. He said the hardest part

was coming off the rim to the Esplanade. The bed of 209 below the Esplanade was easy for him clear to the river, but he recalled the bed being dry.
Butchart and Baxter needed to bypass a fall to the south in the Supai formation.[21]

Farther south in Trail Canyon, Shanley Spring may have provided a mine
with water. Snyder Mine is located above the spring. Ore was hauled down
Trail Canyon by burro and packed out Peach Springs Wash to the railroad.

Walking downstream beyond 209 Mile Canyon becomes increasingly
difficult as the Lower Granite Gorge begins to appear. In many places walking is easier on slopes of Bright Angel Shale above the Precambrian rock.
Below Granite Spring Canyon the southside of the river is easier walking.

220 Mile Canyon

220 Mile Canyon does not have a route from river to the rim that I know
of.

North of Diamond Peak a route through the Redwall will get hikers near
a cave where the Arizona Speleological Society has set up a register.

1 Annerino (1986) p. 299; Brian (1992) p. 117; Aitchinson (1985) pp. 151-153; Kelsey
   (1986); Butchart (1975) p. 29
2 Butchart (1975) p. 30
3 Brian (1992) p. 116
4 *Ibid.*, p. 119
5 *Ibid.*, p. 118
6 *Ibid.*, p. 119
7 Steck (1993) pp. 63-118 [entire narrative is worth reading]
8 Brian (1992) p. 113
9 Brian (1992) p. 113
10 *Ibid.*, p. 107; Granger (1960) p. 19
11 *Ibid.*, p. 139
12 Cox (1973) pp. 33-34, *et al*
13 Bureau of Land Management, "Mount Trumbull Schoolhouse," pp. 1-2
14 Dellenbaugh (1904) p. 30
15 Brian (1992) p. 121
16 Butchart (1975) p. 31
17 Butchart (1975) p. 31
18 Butchart (1975) pp. 31-32
19 Brian (1992) p. 120
20 Butchart (1976) p. 32
21 Butchart (1984) p. 49

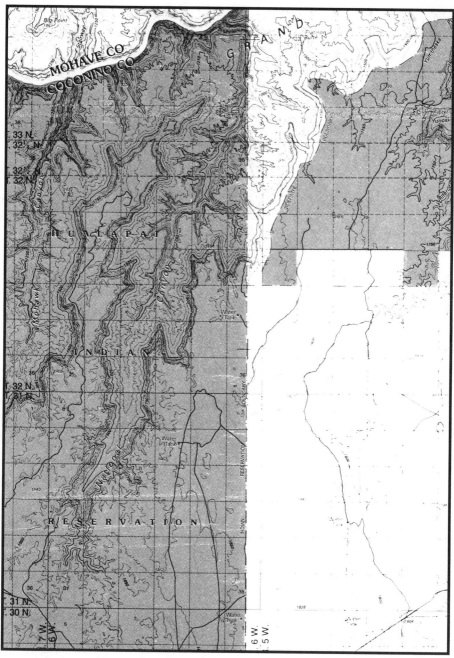

National Canyon area.   Courtesy of Arizona Strip District Bureau of Land Management

Between National and Diamond

Mohawk and National

There are old trails down to the Esplanade in both Mohawk and National. Butchart has described a rope route to the bottom of Mohawk Canyon and Allyn Cureton found a bypass to a fall in National Canyon. Butchart completed his route in National, from rim to river, while on a boat trip with Ken Sleight. He suggests leaning a driftwood log against a cliff to get up the hardest part.[1]

Pot hole water is in the main drainage of National where it crosses the Esplanade and there are seeps in Mohawk Canyon. Ron Beecher, a Hualapai Indian, has walked much of the Esplanade between Prospect Canyon and Supai.

After coming off the rim to the saddle, climbers are able to climb Flat Iron Butte on its east face via a chimney crack. On its summit I experienced a rain storm to the south and clear blue sky on the north half of the peak. During this first ascent, Jim Ohlman nearly stepped on a rattlesnake. The climb was beginning to get tough and we were going back to camp to get more equipment. The Toroweap ledge we were traversing was narrow. I scared up a rattlesnake and it nearly struck Jim who was walking behind me. In a natural reaction to get away from the snake, Jim nearly went off the Coconino cliff.

There is a route to the Esplanade between Cataract Canyon and National Canyon off Yumtheska Point on its western end. Water is available at Pocket Point, north of Flat Iron Butte. Horses graze on the Esplanade in this section of the canyon and they are always a good indication of water nearby.

National Canyon seems to derive its name from the National Forest Service. Before transfer of lands to the Havasupai Tribe, Kaibab National Forest extended to National Canyon.

A few years back, the U. S. G. S. installed a gauging station near the mouth of National Canyon. Shortly afterwards, a low flying helicopter ran into a cable strung across the river and crashed.[2]

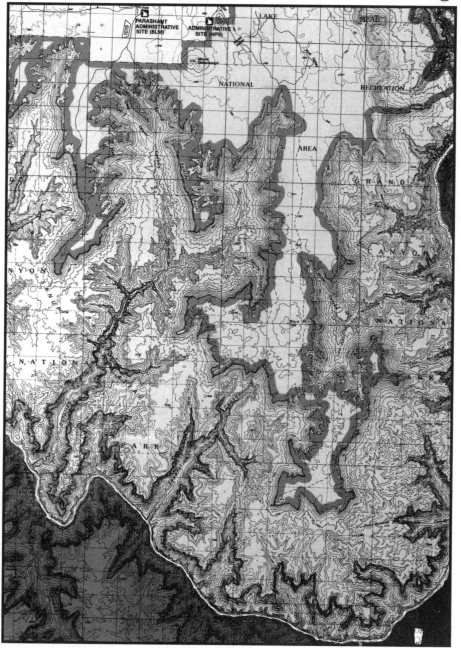

Map Courtesy of Arizona Strip District Bureau of Land Managment

Prospect Valley

Turn off the paved Havasupai Road onto Frazier Wells Road. After about four miles a fork to the left leads to Pine Spring. I have used this fork to Pinnacle Tank for access to Pocomate Springs; although the Prospect Valley Road is better for access. A few miles farther on the Prospect Road a fork to the right leads to the rim above Prospect Valley. At this fork the road to the left goes past Park Tank and begins a descent into Prospect Valley. Immediately to the north of where the road enters the valley stands Prospect Point at 7112 feet. Prospect Point can be climbed via a canyon to its south, or from the rim road on top of the Aubrey Cliffs.

Roads lead all over the place in the Valley. One leads to the DS Ranch in the upper end of Prospect Valley. Another to Mexican Tank and the road into Granite Park. Still another heads towards Prospect Canyon.

Going north, one and a half miles past Twin Tanks a road starts climbing up to the rim above Ridenour Mine and there is an exciting jeep trail down to the Esplanade and the mine. Duard Iverson, while working for Western Gold and Uranium, built the jeep trail during the 1950's when the uranium boom was in full swing. Before the jeep trail was built, another group of men during the 1870's hauled ore from Ridenour Mine by burro.

Slim Stout and I spent the day poking around the mining site looking at the old relics. South of the mine there is a spring on the Esplanade. At one time an airfield was bulldozed across the red shales. Northeast of the mine, and across two unnamed canyons, a bay leads down from the Esplanade to the top of the Redwall. Downstream from Whitmore Rapids, a canyon with a Redwall and Muav route will lead the adventuresome to the river. A route on a ridge offers an interesting alternative for climbers here.

Two and a half miles south of Cement Tank Spring it is possible for hikers to climb out of Prospect Valley, continue over the rim and drop into Hells Hollow. An easier way is to continue on the road, taking the left fork nearest Prospect Canyon. However, this road is rough as it winds across the Esplanade. George Billingsley has located a spring in Hell's Hollow and it is shown on his Geologic Map of Grand Canyon.

193 and 196 Mile Canyons

Below Big Spring it is possible to scramble through the Supai cliffs and then hike down 193 Mile Canyon. The usual access to the Colorado River is via the saddle of 192 Mile Canyon.

East of 193 Mile Canyon the Ridenour Mine makes an interesting 4 x 4 objective. The road off the rim to the mine on the Esplanade is thrilling to say the least. This mine is not as extensive as the one down on Horseshoe Mesa. Ridenour staked claims in Grand Canyon as early as the 1870's. A route to the river off the Esplanade is near, and map study by the hiker should provide enough information.

It most certainly would take several days to hike from Granite Park along the Esplanade to Prospect Canyon.

Both upstream and downstream of 196 Mile Canyon fault line breaks in the limestone cliffs allow access to the Esplanade from the Colorado River. The red rock plateau above the river here is some of the most inaccessible land in the lower 48 states.

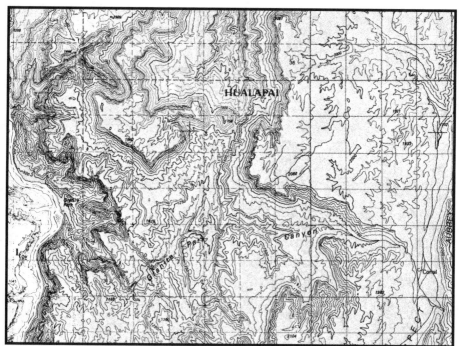

Tommy Mountain.   Map Courtesy Arizona Strip District, Bureau of Land Management

138

Dr. Tommy Mountain and 205 Mile Canyon

This is perhaps the most isolated region in the 48 states. Canyons are dry and hot in the summer with temperatures of over 100 degrees and roads in the winter are accessible to four wheel drive only. The main turnoff for this region of the canyon is off the paved road leading to Supai at Frazier Wells. There is a dirt road that leads back into ponderosa pine trees here. One fork leads to a fire lookout tower near Mohawk Canyon and another fork goes up to the rim above Diamond. If you continue beyond these, the road drops into Prospect Valley. Across the valley a rough road goes to the head of Granite Park.

I have climbed Tommy Mountain (also locally called Hurricane Mesa) several times and it is an easy scramble on its south, east and north sides. The best access is from the Granite Park Esplanade jeep trail.

Preston Nutter horse trail at the head of 193 Mile Canyon provides a way into the canyon farther east. Here a spring is evident where Hermit shale meets Supai formation. Its water is reliable and Jim Ohlman and I spent a cold night there. Someone put in a pipeline to the rim and there are remnants of an old boiler in the drainage.

On the summit of Tommy Mountain are bits and pieces of a plane wreck. As the barometer dropped during a storm the pilot lost visibility and crashed into Tommy Mountain. All passengers and crew died. From the summit hikers get a superb view of Western Grand Canyon.

Climbing out 205 Mile Canyon is not too difficult, but it helps to have a handline along to raise packs. The canyon is dry and there is a long distance between the Colorado River and the spring on the Nutter Trail. During a heavy rainstorm one night many rocks fell near my camp, but the storm provided fresh pot hole water. Mescal pits on the canyon delta in a mesquite thicket show evidence of early man's presence here. One route goes out the north fork of 205 Mile Canyon while another heads up a steep ridge upstream of the delta.

After climbing out the left fork of 205 Mile Canyon, it is possible for a hiker to traverse the Esplanade over to 193 Mile Canyon. An unusual, knee deep snowfall made water no problem one week late in October. Wearing only tennis shoes, I resorted to using bread bags on the outside of my socks to prevent cold injuries. Pilots flying between Las Vegas and Tusayan have reported water pockets on the Esplanade here during the warmer months. Some of the canyons between 205 and 193 Mile Canyon might also provide access to the river.

Granite Park

At Mexican Tank, in Prospect Valley, a road fork leads to the Esplanade in Granite Park. This is a rough road and having four wheel drive is a good idea or hikers may park at the tank and walk down from the rim along the road. On the Esplanade, a jeep trail leads up to Hockey Puck Spring.

It is possible to hike south along the Esplanade from Granite Park to Diamond Creek and there are several breaks in the rim along the way. Hikers have also walked north on the Esplanade to Big Spring above 193 Mile Canyon. A trail heads down to the spring and an alternate trail leaves the rim farther north. Between 193 Mile and Granite Park there is another way to the Esplanade from the rim in a ravine east of X6981.

Colorado River at Granite Park as seen from Tommy Mountain.

At the head of Granite Park several mescal pits provide evidence of Indian presence in the area.

The route in the Redwall formation is south of Tommy Mountain, but north of the main Granite Park drainage.

217 Mile Canyon

Pot Hole Tank is located below the Aubrey Cliffs in the upper valley of Diamond Creek. It was dry in August of 1989, but there was water in Prospect Tank farther north. Southwest of Pot Hole Tank the ground slopes up to the rim of 217 Mile Canyon. There is a break in the rim, south of 7053X, that allows a scramble up to the Esplanade. Although a long hike, the Esplanade does continue between Diamond Creek and Granite Park. It is a solid day from Granite Park across the redrock to 217 Mile Canyon.

Farther down near the river in 217 a fault line (with a displacement of two thousand feet!) leads south up to the saddle of mesa X3697. The cliffs are broken enough to allow hikers access to the Tonto Platform. One side of the saddle is Supai formation, while the other Bright Angel Shale.

Granite Spring Canyon

There is a rugged route from the Colorado River to the rim in Granite Spring Canyon. It is possible to climb out of the Lower Granite Gorge to the Tonto by way of a ridge above saddle X2404. A traverse brought me back into Granite Spring Canyon where it was possible to climb up the Redwall and Supai in a tributary to the north. There is also a route to the rim northeast of the Esplanade here.

Hikers may climb mesa X3697 above the river from the saddle and there are rugged climbing routes around the corner in 217 Mile Canyon.

You can climb peak X5095 high above 224 Mile Canyon. One way into Diamond Creek from Granite Spring is via the saddle northeast of peak X6437 and it is also possible to follow a ridge above the saddle to Sunset Peak (X6543) and the rim.

Upstream on Granite Park delta there are some Indian ruins and mescal pits.

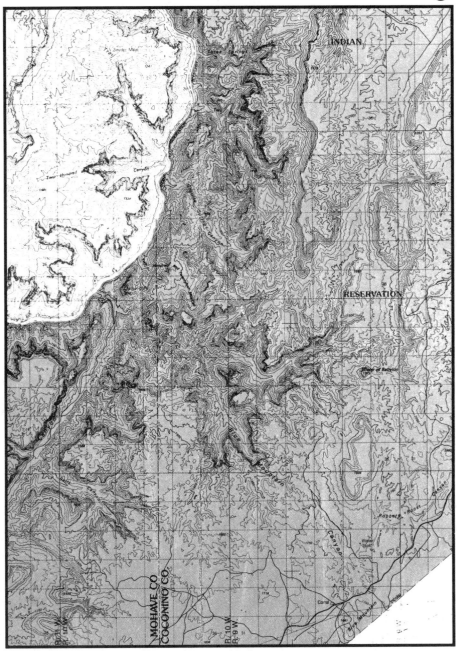

Hualapai Indian Reservation, Peach Springs Wash area.
Map courtesy of Arizona Strip District Bureau of Land Management

Peach Springs

Peach Springs on the Hualapai Indian Reservation is a most interesting place to go hiking and exploring. It is located on old route 66, between Kingman and Seligman. Hualapais charge for hiking but it is worth it.

Joseph Christmas Ives was one of the first recorded white men to reach the river in Grand Canyon. The year was 1858.[3] During the 1880's this was the busiest tourist location in the Grand Canyon region, however that was before the advent of modern highways. When Beale's Survey came here looking for a wagon road to California, the railroad was not far behind.[4] Able to get tourists off the railroad, an early Hotel was established near the confluence of Peach Springs Wash and Diamond Creek, 19 miles north of the town of Peach Springs. Known as the Farley (or Farlee) Hotel, it was destroyed once by a flash flood and later dismantled board by board. Now all that remains is an improved road based on the old Farley stage road.[5] This road stretches for 21 miles and is the only place an automobile may be driven from rim to river at Grand Canyon. Just taking the drive down Peach Springs Wash is worthwhile. It is truly one of the more scenic areas of Grand Canyon.

Farlee Hotel at Diamond Creek.   Mohave County Historical Society

143

There is a small, shaded picnic area above the confluence of Diamond Creek with Peach Springs Wash. The most prominent feature in this area is Diamond Peak. I climbed Diamond Peak and found a bottle with a note in it dating from the 1880's stating that a man and woman climbed the peak together. Perhaps he proposed to her and this is how the peak received the name "Diamond", however the name Diamond Creek existed as early as the Ives Expedition.[5a] From Diamond Creek the route heads east to the saddle. A climber must then traverse ledges to the north side of the peak and begin an ascent up the ridge, weaving a path thru the obstacles as they are met.

It is also possible to reach the river by descending east from Diamond Peak saddle. One can walk many miles along the river upstream not coming to any obstructions until 205 Mile Canyon. George Steck and a number of others have come this way along the river during trans-Canyon treks. Instead of going over Diamond Peak saddle, it is possible to go up to the Tonto level from Diamond Creek and walk above the river on a fairly well defined game trail to the north of Diamond Peak. The Tonto Platform plays out at a faultline where it is but a short distance down a ravine to the Colorado River. I have walked up river to Granite Springs Canyon and climbed a peak with the elevation X4356.

Hikers may also head downstream on the Tonto Platform to Travertine Canyon, by climbing up to the Tonto near the junction of Diamond Creek and Peach Springs Wash. Downriver from Diamond Creek I found climbing to the Tonto difficult. An adventuresome hiker can climb up through the Redwall above Diamond Creek to the west, and also at a place between Diamond and Travertine Canyon. Jim Ohlman suggested a rugged route up the promontory between Diamond Creek and Peach Springs Wash. Farther up Peach Springs Wash I have climbed the "Thumb" on the east face and Ohlman put a rope route down from the saddle on the west side.

For the less hardy, taking a day hike up Diamond Creek narrows makes for an interesting walk. Here the canyon is as narrow and steep as anywhere in the eastern part of Grand Canyon. Some hikers have stated they had trouble with chockstones blocking the "Black Aisle," but I've had no difficulty. Harvey Butchart and Doug Shough also were able to walk up this canyon.[6] Conditions of the stream bed may change from year to year due to flooding. Overnight hikers may continue farther up the canyon by climbing out the Redwall on the right hand side in the main drainage. The route, after a short traverse, will bring you to Diamond Valley on the Esplanade. From here You can climb "Sunset Peak," so called because it may be seen for many miles at sunset. If the pot holes were full of water after some good storms it would be feasible to walk the Esplanade around the base of Sunset Peak, from Diamond Valley to Granite Park jeep trail. It is also possible to head in the opposite direction across the Esplanade toward the Tower of Babylon and "Jim Parker Mesa." There is a jeep trail below the mesa that provides access to the paved Supai Road.

Tower of Babylon has an inscription dated October 1920 at its summit. Robbers Roost Canyon derives its name from Jim Parker who robbed the train in Peach Springs and rode into this canyon. The lawman Asa "Ace" Harris tracked him. There was a shootout but Parker escaped. He was eventually caught near Bitter Springs, Arizona. Locals call the large mesa in Robbers Roost Canyon, "Jim Parker Mesa" and I like to call another peak to the north, "Asa Harris Butte." Both of these peaks are easy scrambles. The "Parker Mesa" saddle will take hikers to the top of the Aubrey Cliffs. The rim above Robbers Roost derived its name from Francois Xavier Aubrey, who set a speed record for riding horses across Arizona. Aubrey was stabbed to death in a barroom brawl.[7] With just a few breaks, the Aubrey Cliffs run more or less continuously from Seligman to Diamond Valley. Robbers Roost Canyon goes over a great fall in the limestone, but it is possible to bypass the fall with a long detour to the right. Some maps call this Blue Mountain Canyon.

Slim Stout and I made a 220 foot rappel in thru the ceiling of a cave in Robbers Roost Canyon and found a room larger than a basketball court. The Speleological Society has a cave register at the base of the rappel. The register calls the cave "Conglomerate."

Hualapai Indians are sometimes known as the "Pine Tree Folk." Their language is similar to Havasupai Indians, to whom they are closely related. Juan de Onate and his soldiers crossed the homeland of the Hualapi people in 1604 and in 1776 Father Garces and his missionaries traveled among them.[8]

1   Butchart (1975) p. 35
2   Brian (1992) p. 114
3   Brian (1992) p. 125; Hughes (1978) p. 28
4   Hughes (1978) p. 28
5   Brian (1992) p. 125
5a   Dellenbaugh (1902) p. 90
6   Butchart (1975) pp. 38-39
7   Brian (1992) p. 118; Trimble (1986)
8   Brian (1992) pp. 10, 98, 157; Hughes (1978) pp. 11-14, 21; Dellenbaugh (1904)
     pp. 76-80, 90-92

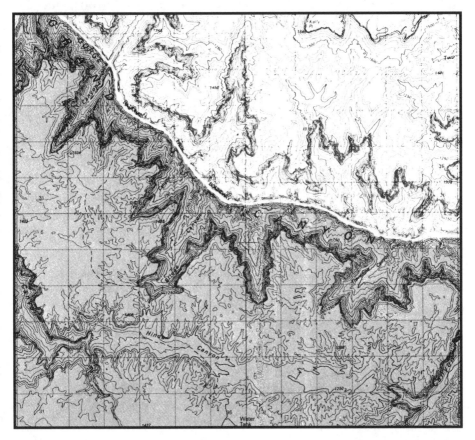

Hindoo Canyon area.

Map courtesy of Arizona Strip District Bureau of Land Management

Lake Mead Southside

Hindoo Canyon

It is about 7 miles from Highway 66 along Buck and Doe Road to a turnoff for Hindoo Canyon. From the fork at Buck and Doe Road it is about 10 miles to Hindoo Canyon. North of the white radio tower the road crosses Plain Flat and having a map can be helpful in finding a correct turnoff for Hindoo and Bridge. The road drops sharply into Hindoo Canyon, becomes very rough and four wheel drive is recommended. Lots of Crucifixion Thorn, Ephedra and Acacia (cat claw) grow here in Hindoo "Valley." It is a little over one mile on foot from where the road leaves the valley to Hindoo Spring. There are several easy falls encountered before the spring is reached. Seep Willows line the spring and its water reliable.

Bridge Canyon; in the distance is the North Rim and Shivwits Plateau. In this part of Grand Canyon the South Rim is comprised of redwall limestone.

147

Bridge Canyon

The road which drops into Hindoo Canyon, crosses that canyon and climbs up to a junction. One fork leads to a canyon vista, while another is the trailhead to Bridge Canyon. The trailhead is unmarked and one must park near a mescal pit on the right hand side of the road above a narrow V-slot drainage. Bridge Canyon Trail initially goes down this canyon. Signs of trail construction are in the form of low walls. It is a short distance before this trail is washed out and hikers must down climb a fall. Using a rope to lower packs is useful. Below this fall a trail is visible again and begins a traverse to the right, below the Redwall cliff. After a short distance the trail descends the canyon in a series of switchbacks (some are vague) down to the drainage bottom where it stays until the Tonto is reached.

Below the Tapeats, a spring in dark precambrian rock provides burros with water. Before reaching the river I was blocked by a high fall in the main drainage. Near the head of the spring I found Robert Benson Eschka's sandals, which sat under a seep willow for a decade.

In places, Jumping Cholla cactus grow on the Tonto in profuse numbers. Hikers should wear long pants and leather shoes to avoid unpleasant encounters. Ephedra, or Mormon tea also dots the slopes. Wild, or feral burros like the habitat, often you will see them grazing near the trail as it makes a way to Separation Canyon.

Gneiss Canyon

There is a small seep in the granite drainage below the Tonto. The Tonto trail coming from the east crosses several mescal pits just before dropping into Gneiss Canyon. The head of the canyon is blocked by a high Redwall cliff. I was unable to reach the river in Gneiss Canyon even after down climbing several waterfalls. I attempted a bypass to the west and found the route to be blocked by an impassable cliff.

On the north side of the Colorado River, across from Gneiss Canyon, an unnamed canyon may hold a route to both Sanup and Shivwits Plateaus.

Bridge Canyon City

The trail continues from Bridge Canyon, west to what river runners call Bridge Canyon City and beyond to Separation Canyon. A number of years ago a dam was proposed for the Colorado River here and some structures were built for a spike camp during the testing of rock at the site.[1] Luckily for canyon hikers the project never materialized and was put on a back burner where it still lies. The spike camp is located in the first small canyon downstream from Gneiss Canyon.

A high fall blocks the elongated arm, but the short arm has a constructed trail down from a promontory dividing the two unnamed canyons. When going down, below a travertine seep, the trail stays on the right hand side of the ravine. Poured concrete slabs, rock walls, heavy cable, a stove, hot water heaters and water pipes still remain today. Usually water is running in the main drainage. This small canyon is very near the head of Lake Mead and rapids on the Colorado River begin to appear above this location.

Separation Canyon (South)

From Bridge Canyon City the trail continues downstream to Separation Canyon along the Tonto Platform. There is no spring in Separation Canyon so hikers must rely on lake water. The bed of Separation is obstacle free until a tamarisk thicket just above the lake. The easiest way around the thicket is on the right side when coming down the drainage. It is easy to put a small backpack raft into the lake at Separation Canyon.

Above the Tonto a way to the rim is blocked by a high fall of several hundred feet in the Redwall cliff. There seems to be no way to the rim between Bridge Canyon and Spencer Canyon. Here Redwall, Temple Butte and Muav walls are definite obstacles.

Downstream of Separation Canyon the constructed trail disappears and hikers must follow a burro trail to Spencer Canyon. Halfway between Separation and Spencer a canyon draining towards the north will access Lake Mead from the Tonto; provided a little route-finding is done. Hikers can also enter Spencer near it's mouth, via a steep Tapeats bay. A rope to lower packs is a must at a chockstone fall along the route.

149

Spencer Canyon

Spencer Canyon is an interesting place to explore. The Buck and Doe Road passes the head of Milkweed Canyon where hikers may park to start a hike. During wet weather this road becomes a mire and having a four wheel drive is a good idea during the winter months.

A ridge between Westwater and Milkweed leads down to the canyon floor just beyond where power lines cross the canyon. I found a burro trail going down the last half of the ridge. Intermittent water seeps are along the canyon bottom with only minor falls to be bypassed. Both the north and south walls of Milkweed Canyon have routes to the rim. Harding Spring fork was wet where it joins Milkweed Canyon; from a distance I saw a route to the rim that might be possible. During December, in the upper end of Milkweed, I leaped down a six foot ledge into a pool of water getting my pants wet. Water was certainly not a problem and I made camp below Harding Spring Canyon. The upper end of Milkweed Canyon has a trail in it and here precambrian rock is reminiscent of Bright Angel area.

Hikers have also come down Hindoo Canyon. Shortly before Hindoo joins Milkweed a high fall must be bypassed. A steep route comes in off the rim of Milkweed south of its mouth. The two canyons join together forming Spencer Canyon. Spencer Canyon was named after Charles Spencer, an early friend of the Hualapai and he is not to be confused with the Spencer of Lee's Ferry. He made his home in the drainages of Spencer Canyon, farmed and even built a rock cabin at Meriwhitica Spring.[2]

The upper end of Spencer is dry until a short distance above the junction with Meriwhitica Canyon. No obstacles block Spencer Canyon and a hiker may walk all the way to the Lake. Lake Mead filled some of the lower canyon, but there is still much to enjoy.

A horse trail comes down Meriwhitica Canyon to Indian Gardens and remains in relatively good condition today. North of the trailhead, across the canyon is a scrambler's route to the rim. In heavy rain and fog I had problems following this route and ended up climbing out a rugged route just west of the monocline.

High above Meriwhitica Spring is a cave that archaeologist Bob Euler spent much time in. The springs' high mineral content raised the level of

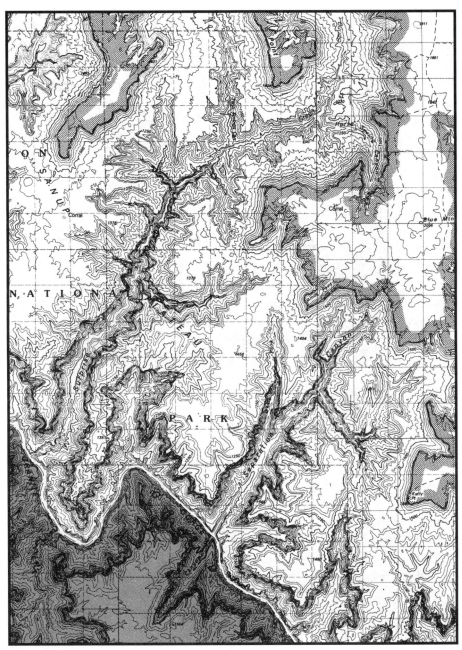

Lake Mead, Separation area.

Map courtesy of Arizona Strip District Bureau of Land Management

151

Meriwhitica Trail; wide and easy to follow.

old irrigation ditches with a platform of limestone-like material, similar to that found in stalagmites. Travertine also formed a large dike near the junction of Spencer and Meriwhitica.[3] After passing an old fence line the trail goes down the southside of the natural dam and continues on to Lake Mead. At the mouth of Spencer it is possible to inflate a small raft, cross the lake, and climb up a ravine to the Tonto on the northside.

To the east of the mouth of Spencer Canyon stand three unnamed peaks that are quite impressive. No one has climbed these summits high above Lake Mead to my knowledge. Hikers refer to them as "Three Sisters." Some folks also refer to these buttes as "Three Bells".

There are still more ways to enter the vast Spencer Canyon drainage. I have climbed out west at the head of Meriwhitica Canyon. From there I was able to hike across the plateau and down the road bed of Clay Springs Canyon. Sometimes water is available at Clay Springs in a stock tank, but it was

152

dry in December of 1994. A rough section of Muav makes 4 x 4 a wise idea on the road in Clay Springs Canyon.

West of Steel Tank another break in rim rock provides access to the canyon bottom of Meriwhitica. Still another route lies west of Spencer Canyon between Milkweed and Meriwhitica Canyon. North of this route is a neat little Redwall butte.

Lost Creek

The rim of the canyon is at the level of the Redwall formation. Easiest access into this area is either by boat from Lake Mead, or via the Buck and Doe Road. For the latter, a turn off for Clay Tank east of where the map shows a Ranger Station; the road will bring hikers into Lost Creek drainage.

Butchart, Pete Eno and I, as well as a number of others have come down this beautiful pristine little canyon. A tributary canyon south of Lost Creek (Clay Tank Canyon) makes this route possible. The route shares a saddle with an unnamed canyon between Lost Creek and Spencer Canyon. Prehistoric man used this route to the river and I found a stone axe head near the top. Butchart found a very large mescal pit at the top of this route.[4] A main food of the early Hualapai Indian was mescal, which they called "viyal." It was taken from the Agave cactus and cooked in a large pit. Wood was laid in the pit and covered with small pieces of rock, then cactus was stacked on top four or five feet high. This was then covered with dirt to keep in the heat. Sometimes mescal was pounded and eaten raw. It was also, soaked in water, and the liquid allowed to partially ferment and used as a drink.

A spring in the drainage near Lake Mead allowed Eno and I to refill our canteens. Vegetation was thick along the creek and the scent of seep willow strong. Underfoot were travertine formations.

Reference Point Creek

Bob Packard succeeded in finding a route down from the rim of Reference Point (Horse Flat Canyon). But, I am not sure of his route down from the rim of this isolated canyon. Map study seems to indicate several possibilities at the canyon head.

153

Lower Granite Gorge, Grand Canyon.
Photo By: Mohave County Historical Society.

An unnamed canyon shares a saddle with Clay Tank Canyon and it is possible to go from one canyon to the other using the saddle. The same fault line that created the saddle also makes a route into Lost Creek possible. Between Reference Point Creek and the unnamed canyon there is a route to the lake from the Tonto.

The spring in the precambrian rock of Reference Point Creek is reliable.

Northern exposure terrain of Hualapai Indian Reservation makes good habitat for sheep. Hikers are more likely to see rams and ewes here than on the north side of Lake Mead, despite competition from feral burros. Increased availability of spring water is also an important factor for their existence.

Quartermaster Canyon

The Buck and Doe Road provides access to the Hualapai Indian Reservation and the south rim of the Grand Canyon above Lake Mead. This is a seldom visited section of the Canyon and its pristine beauty remains relatively

154

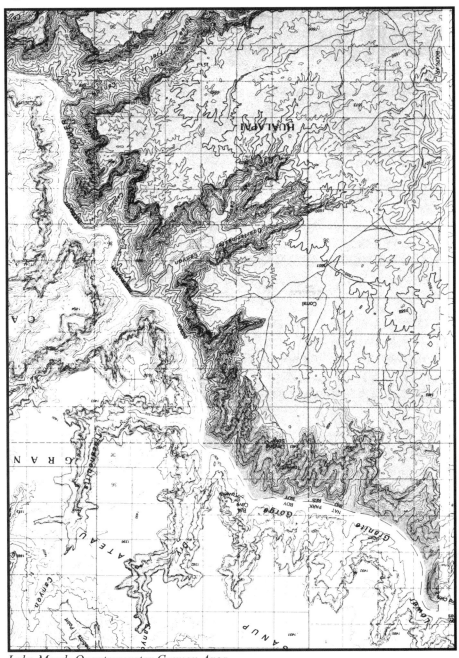

Lake Mead; Quartermaster Canyon Area.

Courtesy of Arizona Strip District Bureau of Land Management

155

untouched. For some geological reason the upper rock formations have eroded on the southside, west of Diamond Creek. The Kaibab, Toroweap, Coconino, Hermit and in many places, the Supai formation, are absent from this part of Grand Canyon. The highest points on the plateau are the Music Mountains and Laughing Jack Butte and they reach up only into the Muav formation.

Quartermaster Canyon is reached by lake or from above off the Buck and Doe Road. The turnoff for the Buck and Doe Road is west of Peach Springs off Old Route 66. Before reaching the Bar Diamond Ranch turnoff there is a rough road that leads to Jeff Tank near the Quartermaster trailhead. An alternate way into this region is Bar Diamond Ranch, off Pearce Ferry Road. Bar Diamond Ranch is located in a canyon near a big curve on Pearce Ferry Road, just south of Meadview.

Named after a Hualapai Indian, Quartermaster Canyon contains a number of archeological sites.[5] Many young Hualapai men acted as scouts for the army in the early days frontier of the Arizona Territory.[6] To enter Quartermaster Canyon hikers must first climb up to the base of the Redwall before descending from the rim. The trail is vague and not shown on topographical maps. The faint trail switchbacks down the Muav formation to the canyon floor. Following the canyon bottom to the lake is easy from here. Depending on the level of Lake Mead it is sometimes easier to moor a boat downriver against a Tapeats ledge. Tonto Platform again becomes pronounced in this section of the canyon and burro trails lead off in both directions. To the upstream side of Quartermaster there is a large travertine deposit, riddled with small caves. Also a number of small springs are in the area.

North of Quartermaster Canyon there is a large mesa X4952 and I do not know of anyone having ever climbed it. Southeast is Jackson Canyon, which is about a days walk from Quartermaster along the Tonto Platform. There is also a route to Lake Mead in Jackson Canyon from the Tonto. Walking along the Tonto northwest is very easy for several miles along an old burro trail, and climbers might still discover a rim-to-lake route between Cave Canyon and Quartermaster.

Cave Canyon

Located near the mouth of Cave Canyon, Rampart Cave contains pre-historic records of huge sloths that roamed this part of Arizona 30,000 years ago.[7] Park Service has erected a wrought iron gate with a lock to protect the cave from vandals. There is evidence of early man as well, as I found fragments of a pot in Cave Canyon under an overhang.

There are two barrier falls at the Lower end of Cave Canyon, which are passed in opposite directions. In his book Butchart noted a shelter cave where Belknap and Visbak saw artifacts. Visbak and Belknap went down from near New Water Spring via the east arm passing the shelter cave on the West.[8]

I spent several nights in Cave Canyon and it is a most interesting place to explore. Columbine Falls pours into Lake Mead and is a year round source of fresh water. West of Columbine Falls a small canyon leads to the south where a hiker could climb out to the top of the Grand Wash Cliffs. The upper part of the route follows a ridge west of X4752.

From New Water Spring, a route heads down the central fork of Cave Canyon to the upper valley below the Redwall formation. Farther down, saddles are shared in two places with an unnamed canyon to the east. It would be interesting to see if a route will go to the lake via one of these.

East of the Ferry several sheep trails go to the top of the Grand Wash Cliffs. Another route, into Cave Canyon, is in a small bay east of a peak with elevation 4202. The ridge that divides Grapevine Wash from Cave Canyon also provides a route to the south rim.

157

Former location of Pearce Ferry before the waters of Lake Mead covered it.
Photo: 1923 USGS   Grand Canyon National Park #17104

Pearce Ferry

By far the best road to Pearce Ferry is the paved road between Dolan Springs and Meadview. The last eight miles are gravel, but the road still is accessible to passenger cars. Alternate routes into the area are Stockton Hill Road leaving Kingman and Pearce Ferry Road off old U.S. Route 66.

Meadview has a store and a gas station that provide service for the fishermen. From Meadview a jeep trail goes down Grapevine Wash to the lake. Standing in downtown Meadview a hiker will notice several ways up east through the Grand Wash Cliffs. One route heads up to the saddle of an unnamed peak with the triangulation station "Vine." Another tops out northwest of New Water Tank. Using these game trails it is possible to head north towards pothole water and a spring in Cave Canyon. Once while hiking up to the top of these cliffs I came across a herd of 30 bighorn sheep. They like the water sources, and rugged canyons in the Grand are good protection from a hunter's bullets. This part of Grand Canyon National Park is administered via a Ranger Station at Meadview, where a ranger usually is on duty.

At the base of the Grand Wash Cliffs, the Muddy Creek formation holds what geologists believe are keys to the formation of Grand Canyon. Billingsley, Huntoon and Clark have dated these deposits as Tertiary in age.[9] It is also possible to hike along the lake water line to the mouth of Cave Canyon or even as far as Quartermaster Canyon. But ledges are so steep one must take care.

Below Pearce Ferry, the Powell Expedition was guided by a manuscript journal which Jacob Hamblin and two other Mormons, Miller and Crosby, had kept on a boat journey a few years earlier from Grand Wash to Callville. Ives and others having been up to Callville, the exploration of the Colorado River by 1869 was complete and no part of it unknown.[9a]

Music Mountains

Music Mountains are the southernmost end of Grand Wash Cliffs. Visible from Kingman, the white striped cliffs received their name from an early prospector who said when the wind blew he heard the sound of musical instruments.[10] Deer abound in this range and water is available for wildlife at stock tanks and Black Spring.

A good way to access this area of the Hualapai is to leave Highway 66 near Truxton. A day hike will take you to the summit of Laughing Jack Butte, named after a Hualapai Indian Chief.[11] The view on top is worthwhile, and even though there is no trail, novice hikers should find no problem attaining the summit. The easiest routes are between the comb like peaks.

Below Laughing Jack Butte are the towns of Truxton and Hackberry, which in the 1850's were the scene of a massacre.[12] To retaliate, blue coats under command of Major Redwood Price fought a band of Indians on the north end of the Music Mountains where the mountain range meets the western valley floor. Artifacts from the fight can still be found. Raiding a shipment of supplies, Indians took a captured wagon and burned it in Clay Springs Canyon.[13] Elmer Butler once found twenty blue coats (without buttons) in a cave near this location. Perhaps the Indians liked the shine of the buttons. Clay Springs Canyon has a stock tank which sometimes has water, and dirt road provides easiest access to Spencer Canyon Trail.

The summit of Laughing Jack Butte is Muav formation and the Tonto continues uninterrupted by roads to the west above Flat Rock Spring. The Tonto Platform then swings north to Black Mesa and the head of Milkweed Canyon. This bench is forested with piñon and juniper. Walking is quite easy here. Occasionally you get a glimpse of antelope browsing vegetation.

The Hualapai Indians were still using arrow points made of stone as late as 1871.[14] Points were made of obsidian, chert and other hard stones. But in this part of the canyon chert seems the most popular.

Music Mountains as seen from Truxton, off U.S. 66; Hualapai Indian Reservation boundary fence in the foreground.

1   Butchart (1975) pp. 41-42; Brian (1992) p. 127
2   Butchart (1975) pp. 42-43; Brian (1992) p. 128
3   Butchart (1975) p. 43; Brian (1992) p. 129
4   Butchart (1975) pp. 55-57
5   Brian (1992) pp. 130-131; q.v. Butchart (1975) pp. 43-45
6   Hughes (1978) p. 29
7   Brian (1992) pp. 132-133; q.v. Butchart (1975) p. 45; q.v. Stevens (1993) p. 105; Hughes (1978) p. 93
8   Butchart (1984) pp. 63-64; q.v. Butchart (1975) p. 45
9   Beus and Morales (1990)
9a Dellenbaugh (1902) pp. 230-231
10 C.F. Granger (1985) p. 217
11 Mohave County Historical Society Archives
12 Mohave County Historical Society Archives
13 Mohave County Historical Society Archives
14 Mohave County Historical Society Archives, "The Walapai Papers."

Sanup Plateau; Lake Mead

Map courtesy of Arizona Strip District Bureau of Land Management

162

Lake Mead Northside

Separation Canyon

At the mouth of Separation Canyon a plaque on the downstream cliff commemorates Powell's Expedition. The Howland brothers and William Dunn opted to leave the expedition here in 1869. They were given two rifles, a shotgun and planned to forage for their food. Jack Sumner gave one of the Howlands his watch. Later, Jacob Hamblin learned from Utes farther east the three men were killed by the Shivwits band.[1]

The west fork of Separation Canyon is blocked by a high cliff, but the east fork leads to the rim. Wet weather pockets are in the main bed at the level of the Muav formation, and perhaps Dunn and the Howlands filled their canteens here.

There is shade on Shivwits Plateau at Dinner and Ambush Water Pockets. Ambush is quite large and a year round water source. Access to this area requires a four wheel drive and is still some of the most isolated country in the lower 48 states. Slim Stout, Glen Henshaw and I hiked off the road from our vehicle to Ambush Water Pocket. Slim searched for artifacts and bullet marks on rocks while I filled our canteens. Glen imitated the men being killed by Indians. It would be interesting to locate an old fire ring at Dinner Pockets; it is said Howlands and Dunn stopped there before being ambushed.

Surprise Canyon

You can hike from river to rim in Surprise Canyon without much difficulty. Its mouth is so narrow that boaters may miss it as they are going up the lake. There is an old constructed trail off Twin Point and it is possible to go down a canyon through the Redwall southeast of this. The Redwall requires some scouting, but a route to the canyon bottom is not difficult. Going to the lake is an easy hike from here, and intermittent water occurs in the main drainage of Surprise Canyon.

Two routes off the rim to Sanup Plateau are possible in Twin Creek

163

and Twin Spring Canyons. After climbing out Twin Spring Canyon I headed east and climbed to the top of Mount Dellenbaugh. Frederick S. Dellenbaugh was the youngest member of Powell's second Colorado River expedition. He was hired on at the age of seventeen as a boatman by Powell after a personal interview. Dellenbaugh afterward wrote: "Of course I was much pleased at having my name thus perpetuated. The mountain turned out to be the culminating point of the Shewits Plateau. None of us visited it at that time, but Thompson went there later, and I crossed its slopes twice several years afterward. On the summit is a circular ruin about twenty five feet in diameter with walls remaining two feet high."[2]

Butchart knows of a route leaving the rim near Amos Point dropping down to Sanup Plateau. He also proposed a Redwall route a little over a mile downstream from the junction of Green Spring Canyon with Surprise Canyon.[3]

It is possible to hike both upstream and downstream along the level of the Tonto from Surprise Canyon. A scramble route from the Tonto to Lake Mead is opposite Spencer Canyon. Farther uplake, another route is near the mouth of the first unnamed canyon beyond Surprise Canyon.

Downstream from the mouth of Surprise Canyon, on a ridge high above Lake Mead, mesa X4432 would make an interesting objective for canyon buffs. I do not know of anyone who has stood on this ridgeline.

Burnt Spring Canyon

Once, while hiking up this canyon from Lake Mead, I found a stone metate under an overhang near its mouth. Farther up I found remnants of sandals woven from brush in a shallow cave. Cattle roam free in this part of Grand Canyon and there is a cattle trail which comes down the straight fork of Burnt Spring Canyon. Near the lake there is a spring in the canyon wash and a wet weather seep on Sanup Plateau. Red Rock Spring seems to be a seasonal seep just below Sanup Plateau, but a cliff blocks progress to it.

You can hike the Sanup Plateau in both directions and climb the small peak immediately west of Burnt Spring Canyon which the map refers to as

Red Point. From the unmapped seep on the Sanup Plateau it is possible to climb to the top of Shivwits Plateau via the left fork to a forest access road on the rim.

Farther upstream near the lake, Salt Canyon has paintings under a cliff overhang that might indicate an ancient route out of this canyon. Drawn with red hematite, an ear of corn is depicted. Perhaps the Redwall formation is broken up enough in Salt to allow passage to Sanup Plateau.

Tincanebitts Canyon

It is over 80 miles of rough road across the Arizona Strip to trailheads above Lake Mead end of Grand Canyon. Easier access is by way of boat from Pearce Ferry.

I have failed to climb out of both Bat Cave Canyon and Tincanebitts. The latter did have a smoke stained overhang near the first fork above the lake indicating the early Indians used this canyon. Billingsley's geologic map of the canyon seems to indicate a route up this fork.[4] Perhaps further exploration of these two will net someone a route to the rim of the Sanup and farther up to Shivwits Plateau. This could be the route that Butchart and Bruce Braley used; it is described in Grand Canyon Treks III.

I have come down from Shivwits Plateau via Tincanebitts Canyon to Sanup Plateau in five different places. Joe Spring may have water; but its realibility is questionable.

Dry Canyon has a route down the fork from Shivwits west of Tincanebitts Tank to Sanup Plateau. I found no water on the Sanup Plateau around Dry Canyon. Jorgen Visbak and I passed this way on our hike between Burnt Spring and Snap Canyons. A dry fall of the Sanup rim makes this canyon seemingly impossible for a ropeless route to Lake Mead; however the west fork may offer strong climbers a rugged way.

South of the mouth of Tincanebits Canyon, on Sanup Plateau are two mesas that to my knowledge have not been climbed. I have stood on the ridge that separates Burnt Spring Canyon from Tincanebitts and taken a close look at the large mesa. There could be a route on the south side off the Sanup rim, but reaching the saddle may have to be done on the north side of the ridge.

Guano Mine Tramway on "Batchit" Point.
Photo By: Mohave County Historical Society.

A trail goes up slope to an old mine at the Bat Cave and one must climb up a long steel ladder to get inside the cave. Bat guano was the "ore" mined here and it was used for high grade fertilizer. Ore was taken to the rim by tram and several towers still stand on the south side of Lake Mead on Bat Chit Point. It takes some confidence to climb up the tall steel ladder leading up to the cave.[5]

Pearce Canyon

After crossing the lake from Pearce Ferry, it is possible for a hiker to climb up to Sanup and Shivwits Plateaus via both Snap Canyon and Pearce Canyon. The latter has mescal pits and old Indian paintings indicating Pearce Canyon was a major route for early man. I found several of these mescal pits on a saddle of an unnamed peak near the mouth of Pearce Canyon. John Wesley Powell noted prospector's burros here in 1869 during his first expedition down the Colorado River.[6]

There are several ways to climb out of Pearce Canyon and hikers usually do not have a problem with route finding here. It seems easiest to stay in the main drainage all the way to just below Fort Garrett. There are several overhangs along the way which contain Indian paintings. South of Pearce Canyon several sheep trails lead up to a large mesa X4745. On top of Sanup Plateau there is an unusual depression that is quite large. Perhaps it's the result of collapse of a large cavern below the surface. George Billingsley calls this the "Grand Pipe."[7]

Fort Garrett is an old rock walled structure that sits on Sanup Plateau and it provided early prospectors and cowboys with shelter. No one has yet put a date on the structure.[8] Sanup, according to Arizona historians, is a Paiute word meaning "male squaw." Shivwits Plateau derives its name from a band of Paiute Indians that lived in the area.[9]

It is possible to scramble to the basaltic summit of Snap Point via Pearce Canyon but one must bypass a cliff. I made a false start before doubling back to the correct route. The view on top is unique to Grand Canyon as the Colorado Plateau comes to an abrupt end.

Snap Canyon

Jorgen Visbak and I walked Sanup Plateau from Snap Canyon to Tincanebitts Canyon. There are springs in Snap Canyon just above the Sanup and seasonal water is available around Pearce.

Northwest of Snap Canyon it is possible to climb Nevershine on the southern side, and from Nevershine you can climb up to Sanup Plateau above Snap Canyon. Where Cunningham Canyon enters Snap it is also possible to climb up a ridge that divides the two canyons. From the top it is only a short distance to the jeep trail on the Sanup. There is an old copper mine in Cunningham Canyon.

North of Snap Point a jeep trail winds across Sanup Plateau from Fort Garrett to Pigeon Canyon and beyond. Pigeon Canyon has a mine and a rugged jeep trail in the Redwall.[10] Some of these jeep trails are washed out in the area of Grand Gulch and impassable to vehicles. Three springs provide water in upper Pigeon Canyon.

A road also comes down Jump Canyon from the Arizona Strip into the drainage of the Grand Wash. Water flowing from springs in Jump Canyon during middle of the summer is not unusual.

Grand Wash

A road comes into Grand Wash from Bunkerville, Nevada but one must leave the Interstate 15 at Mesquite in order to reach the road. The easiest access to Grand Wash Wilderness Area seems to be the road through Whitney Pass. Another road comes up from Mesquite, Nevada via Elbow Canyon, but the road has several rough sections and requires four wheel drive. After climbing out of Elbow Canyon the road passes Cougar Spring and Mount Bangs (Hancock Peak) trailhead. It is about three miles of trail to the top of this peak and the view is spectacular. There are also other hiking trails in the area.

Road leading into Grand Wash from Mesquite, Nevada via Lime Kiln Canyon; note snow in foreground.

Several trails lead to the top of Mount Bangs (Hancock Peak). The easiest and shortest leaves the trailhead at Cougar Spring. The distance is about three miles to the peak. I had problems finding the trail and ended up on one leading to some prospects. It was necessary to bust a lot of brush for about 1,000 feet of elevation to the peak. There is some mild bouldering and route finding near the top. On the summit are some splendid views of the Nevada desert. Zion, Pine Valley Mountain in Utah, Grand Wash and Cerbat Mountains of Arizona are also visible. Brown Bear Mountaineering Club of California established a summit register and it is getting to have quite a list of names. An old triangulation tripod lies near the summit and a marker calls the mountain Hancock Peak. Ponderosa pine trees grow near the top along with Douglas fir trees on northern exposure slopes.

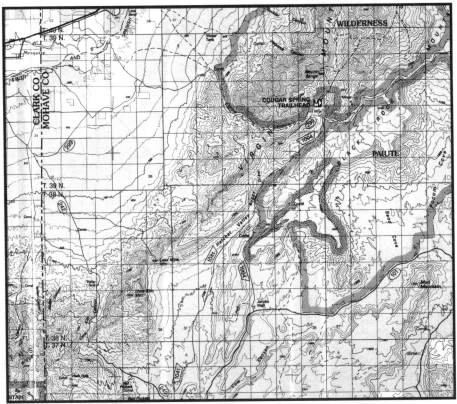

Mesquite, Nevada and the Virgin Mountains.

Map courtesy of Arizona Strip District Bureau of Land Management

169

Still another road leaves Mesquite going south up Lime Kiln Canyon. The road is only a little better and I would advise using four wheel drive. Lime Kiln Mountain is easily climbed from the south, but the northern buttress of Redwall limestone may offer a technical challenge to climbers. A BLM sign says the elevation is 4880 where the road tops out at the saddle. Red Permian shale and Toroweap formation is on the right when you reach Lime Kiln saddle. Toroweap limestone is dated by Geologists at approx: 250 million years of age. From the top of Lime Kiln Canyon it is four miles by road to Brumely Well. Above Brumely Well a cattle trail climbs Red Pockets Mountain via its southern slope. From the summit Grand Wash Bay of Lake Mead is visible.

Old corral in Cottonwood Wash; the road ends at this point.

Heading south from Brumely Well junction by road will bring one to Grand Wash. From Brumely Well a fork to the west goes seven miles to Whitney Pass and back to Bunkerville, Nevada. The left fork will take one to Mount Bangs trailhead and Elbow Canyon.

A junction at Allan Well leads north and climbs up onto Sanup Plateau below Hidden Rim.

Cottonwood Wash makes for a short but interesting day hike. I found room outlines on top of the peak above the mouth of Cottonwood. Ranger Walker of the Arizona Strip District said he knew of a place where corn was ground near there. Perhaps dry farming of corn took place here in iron rich red soil.[11] In Cottonwood Canyon there is a spring and a corral. Several miles above the spring a jeep trail comes down from Black Rock Mountain to upper Cottonwood, but goes no farther.

A fork south of Allan Well leads down to Grand Wash Bay on Lake Mead. I have driven this road and it is over fifty miles from I-15 to Lake Mead below Tassi Spring. Cocks Comb stands above the mouth of Grand Wash. A ranch in the valley near Tassi Spring was built in 1903 from driftwood logs that came down the Colorado River. Cocks Comb has a counterpart on the southside of the lake known as Wheeler Ridge. I once saw three bighorn sheep while hiking on Wheeler above Twin Coves. Cocks Comb of Grand Wash looks much like the one west of House Rock Valley near the Buffalo Ranch.

The Grand Wash Wilderness is an interesting place to go hiking. A foot trail goes across the Sanup Plateau, leaving just north of Squaw Canyon and finishing below Hidden Rim. After leaving the road east of Olaf Knolls there are many ways to hike up through the Redwall to the top of the Sanup Plateau.

171

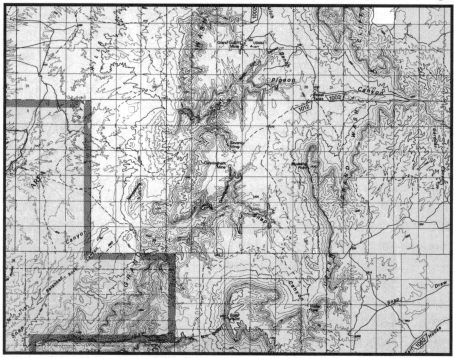

Snap Point and the Grand Wash Cliffs.

Map Courtesy Arizona Strip District Bureau of Land Management

1   Dellenbaugh (1904) pp. 226-230; q.v. Powell (1961); Brian (1992) pp. 127-128; Hughes
    (1978) p. 35
2   Dellenbaugh (1904) p. 310; q.v. Brian (1992) p. 121
3   Butchart (1984) pp. 52-55
4   Huntoon and Billingsley (1982)
5   Brian (1992) p. 131
6   Powell (1961)
7   Huntoon and Billingsley (1982)
8   Trimble (1986)
9   Brian (1992) p. 142, also p. 140
10 Mitchell (1983)
11 In conversation with Ranger Walker, of the B.L.M. Arizona Strip District I learned of evidence that
    he had found indicating that Indians ground their corn in the area of the Grand Wash.

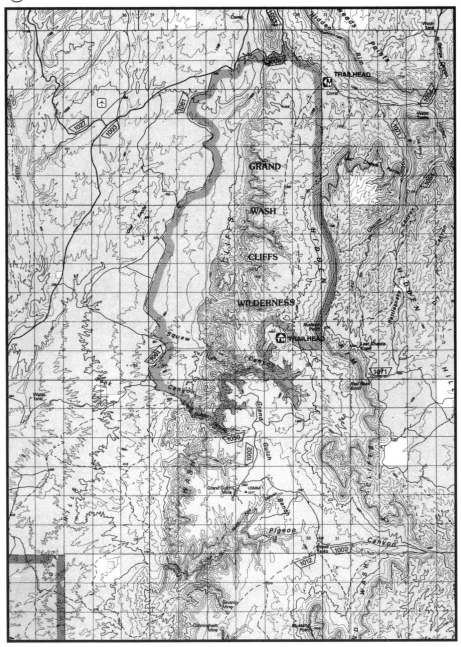

Grand Wash Cliffs Wilderness

Map courtesy of Arizona Strip District Bureau of Land Management

John Hance leading a group of three down Bright Angel Trail on Mules, June, 1902.
Photo By: Peabody   Grand Canyon National Park #823

Annotated Bibliography

Aitchinson, Stewart, 1985 A Naturalist's guide to hiking the Grand Canyon. Englewood Cliffs, NJ: Prentice-Hall, Inc., 172 pp. [A good guide to some of the more scenic parts of the Grand Canyon, complete with road logs to the less visited trailheads]

Aitchinson, S., and Grubbs, Bruce, 1991 The hiker's guide to Arizona. Helena, MT: Falcon Press Publishing Co., Inc., 2nd ed., 237 pp. [General guide covering parts of the entire state. Grand Canyon hikes on pp. 21-39. Curious inclusion of Blue Springs and Surprise Canyon routes, as these are not for the average hiker]

Anderson, M. F., 1992 "Bright Angel and Colorado River Trails History," unpub. manuscript (February 1992) [This paper, along with the two which follow are available at the NPS library, Grand Canyon]

Ibid., 1991a "Human History of the Thunder River Trail in Grand Canyon," unpub. manuscript (December, 1991)

Ibid., 1991b "North and South Bass Trails Historical Research Study, Grand Canyon National Park, Arizona," Cooperative agreement sponsored by the U. S. Department of the Interior, NPS and the Center for Colorado Plateau Studies, Northern Arizona University (Summer, 1991)

Annerino, John, Hiking the Grand Canyon, Sierra Club Books, San Francisco, CA, 1986. 340 pp. [There's a whole lot jammed in this little book! Good for escape routes from the River. Many errors in the list of climbed summits, however]

Arizona State Parks Association, 1990 (2nd ed.) Arizona State Trails Guide. Phoenix, AZ [A 3-ring binder full of mostly short dayhikes. Statewide trail coverage]

Babbitt, James E., and Thybony, Scott, 1991 A Guide to the South and North Bass Trails. Grand Canyon Natural History Association, 48 pp. (including covers). [Grand Canyon Trail Guide Series. The pamphlets in this series are "trail-specific," and are good introductions to the human and natural history of each trail]

Belknap, William, III, 1969 Grand Canyon river guide. Salt Lake City, UT: Canyonlands Press, Special River Runners Waterproof, 48 pp.

[The first and still one of the best]

Berkowitz, Alan, 1979 Guide to the Bright Angel Trail. Grand Canyon Natural History Association, 24 pp. (including covers). [Grand Canyon Trail Guide Series]

Berkowitz, Alan, 1980 Guide to the North Kaibab Trail. Grand Canyon Natural History Association. [Grand Canyon Trail Guide Series]

Beus, S. S., and Morales, M. (eds.), 1990 Grand Canyon Geology. New York and Oxford: Oxford University Press and Museum of Northern Arizona, 518 pp. [Although not specifically written for the layman, this book covers all aspects of the geological development of Grand Canyon and is the best single source for this information]

Brian, Nancy, 1992 River to Rim: A guide to place names along the Colorado River in Grand Canyon, from Lee's Ferry to Lake Mead. Flagstaff, AZ: Earthquest Press, 176 pp. [Until this book came along, the best sources for Grand Canyon place name information were the exhaustive works by Byrd Granger and Will C. Barnes. This is now the best, and it is loaded with source references for those wishing to delve further into this subject]

Brooks, Juanita, 1950 The Mountain Meadows massacre. Stanford University Press, 253 pp. [Although not the last word on J. D. Lee and his role in this tragedy, it is certainly one of the most readable]

Pearce Ferry Landing.
Photo By: Mohave County Historical Society

Burak, Gale "All about a Tree and a Pot." *O'Pioneer* (Newsletter of the Grand Canyon Pioneers Society). [Past issues of this newsletter are available through the Special Collections and Archives section of the Cline Library, Northern Arizona University, Flagstaff, AZ]

Butchart, Harvey, 1960 "Backpacking on the Colorado." *Appalachia,* n. s., V. 26, pp. 176-182. [for years Harvey used a flimsy air mattress in his river crossings and downriver float trips, but since the installation of Glen Canyon Dam, the Colorado River is too cold to safely use this equipment. Two-man rubber { or heavy plastic} rafts are now considered the gear of choice]

----------, 1965a "The Lower Gorge of the Little Colorado." *Arizona Highways,* V. 41, pp. 34-42. (Sept., 1965) [To date, the best guide and historic summary for "trails" in the L. C. Gorge]

----------, 1965b "Wotans Throne." *Summit,* V. 11, pp. 8-11 (Sept., 1965) [Follows the historical development of human visitation on this "sky island"]

----------. 1976 Grand Canyon Treks; a guide to the Inner Canyon routes. Glendale, CA: La Siesta Press, 72 pp. [first published in 1970, this guide, along with its two companion volumes, is a highspeed romp through the wilds of the Grand Canyon "outback." Harvey's books are classics, but they should be used to provide incentive and motivation rather than actual guidance. This volume covers the heart of the Grand Canyon.]

Butchart, J. H., 1975 Grand Canyon Treks II; a guide to the extended canyon routes. Glendale, CA: La Siesta Press, 48 pp. [Covers Marble Canyon and Western Grand Canyon]

Butchart, J. H., 1984 Grand Canyon Treks III; Inner Canyon Journals. Glendale, CA: La Siesta Press, 72 pp. [Covers specific routes and trips throughout the entire Grand Canyon]

Butchart, Harvey (nd) Flagstaff, AZ: Northern Arizona University, Special Collections, Cline Library [a collection of Harvey's Grand Canyon hiking logs dating from 1940's to 1990's. Bound in four volumes]

Casanova, Frank E., 1967 "Trails to Supai in Cataract Canyon." *Plateau,* V. 39, pp. 124-130 [Excellent historical coverage, especially of the less known trails]

Collier, Michael, 1980 An Introduction to Grand Canyon Geology. Grand Canyon Natural History Association, 48 pp. [The best book on the subject for the non-geologist]

Cox, Nellie I., 1973 Footprints on the Arizona Strip, Bountiful, UT: Horizon Publishers. [This book, along with a companion volume titled "Harsh Land and Proud, are classic accounts of pioneer life on the Arizona Strip]

Crumbo, Kim, 1981 A river runner's guide to the history of the Grand Canyon. Boulder, CO: Johnson Books, 61 pp. [A good guide to the history, if not the river itself. Good bibliography]

Dellenbaugh, Frederick S., 1904 The Romance of the Colorado River. Chicago, IL: Rio Grand Press, 399 pp. [A classic written by a member of Powell's second Colorado River expedition]

Dellenbaugh, Frederick S., 1902 The Romance of the Colorado River, G. P. Putnam's Sons, New York and London, The Knickerbocker Press, 399 pp. [Earlier edition]

Fletcher, Colin, 1967 The Man Who Walked Through Time. New York, NY: Alfred A. Knopf. [A long narrative on one mans' physical and mental journey through the heart of Grand Canyon]

Garrison, L. A., 1949 "John Hance: Guide, Trailbuilder, Miner and Windjammer of the Grand Canyon." *Arizona Highways,* V. 25, pp. 4-11 (June, 1949)

Granger, Byrd, 1960 Grand Canyon Place Names. Tucson, AZ: University of Arizona Press, 27 pp. (including inside front cover) [This is an extract from a much longer work on Arizona place names by Byrd Granger. She revised and updated Will C. Barnes's book on the subject, and both should be consulted as authoritative references]

Hamblin, W. K., and Rigby, J. K., 1968 Guidebook to the Colorado River, Part 1: Lee's Ferry to Phantom Ranch in Grand Canyon National Park; with notes on aboriginal cultures by R. T. Matheny, and on biological features by J. R. Murphy. Brigham Young University Geologic Studies, (15)5, Studies for Students, (4) 84 pp. [This book, along with its companion, are unique in that they were the first River guides to utilize aerial photographs. This has made determination of ones' location along the River an easy task, and in my estimation, has greatly increased the value and usefulness of the guide, especially for those hiking in Marble Canyon]

Hamblin, W. K., and Rigby, J. K., 1969 Guidebook to the Colorado River, Part 2: Phantom Ranch in Grand Canyon National Park to Lake Mead, Arizona-Nevada. Brigham Young University Geologic Studies, (16)2, Studies for Students, (5), 126 pp.

Henry, Marguerite, 1991 (Originally published in 1953) Brighty of the Grand Canyon. New York, NY: Aladdin Books, 223 pp. [A cute story about a misplaced mule]

Hirst, Stephen, 1985 Havasu 'Baaja: People of the Blue Green Water.' Supai, AZ: The Havasupai Tribe, 259 pp. [An excellent historical and cultural history of the Havasupai]

Houk, Rose, 1981 Guide to the South Kaibab Trail. Grand Canyon Natural History Association [Grand Canyon Trail Guide Series]

Hughes, J. Donald, 1978 In the house of stone and light; a human history of the Grand Canyon. Grand Canyon Natural History Association, 137 pp. [The best and most complete historical summary of Grand Canyon available. This should be on the book shelf of every Grand Canyonophile] (reprint edition)

Huntoon, P. W., Billingsley, G. H., Breed, W. J., *et al,* 1976 Geologic Map of Grand Canyon National Park. Grand Canyon Natural History Association and Museum of Northern Arizona, scale 1:62,500 [This map and the 1981 and 1982 maps which follow are the best geologic maps available for this vast area]

Huntoon, P. W., Billingsley, G. H., 1977 Geological map of Western Grand Canyon, Arizona. Grand Canyon Natural History Association Open File, 43 sheets [These are the individual 7.5 minute quadrangles which were compiled to create the three large-format geologic maps of the entire Grand Canyon]

Huntoon, P. W., Billingsley, G. H., with Clark, Malcolm D., 1981 Geologic Map of the Hurricane Fault Zone and Vicinity, Western Grand Canyon, Arizona. Grand Canyon Natural History Association, scale 1:48,000

Huntoon, P. W., Billingsley, G. H., with Clark, Malcolm D., 1982 Geologic Map of the Lower Granite Gorge and Vicinity, Western Grand

Canyon, Arizona. Grand Canyon Natural History Association, scale 1:48,000

Illif, F. G., 1985 People of the Blue Water; A record of life among the Walapai and Havasupai Indians. Tucson, AZ: University of Arizona Press, 271 pp. (reprint edition)

James, G. W., 1900 In and Around the Grand Canyon. Boston, MA: Little, Brown and Co., 341 pp. [A seminal work by a turn of the century guidebook author and inveterate wanderer. Note, however, that the author has a certain bias for W. W. Bass]

Kelsey, Michael R., 1987 Hiking and exploring the Paria River. Provo, UT: Kelsey Publishing, 208 pp. [The best there is on the subject]

----------, 1986 Canyon hiking guide to the Colorado Plateau. Provo, UT: Kelsey Publishing, 256 pp. [Kelsey's shotgun approach to hiking and writing and his perverse adherence to the metric system of measurement may irritate some readers, but this guidebook is loaded with good ideas, and should be consulted before venturing far afield]

Lavender, David, 1985 River Runners of the Grand Canyon. Grand Canyon Natural History Association and University of Arizona Press, Tucson, AZ, 147 pp. [Once again, the best reference on the subject, although some might disagree...]

Mckee, E. D., Ancient Landscapes of the Grand Canyon Region. Flagstaff, AZ: Northland Press [reprinted often since 1931. A good little book, although superseded now by the efforts of Collier, Beus and Morales]

Measeles, Evely B., 1981 Lee's Ferry: a crossing on the Colorado. Boulder, CO: Pruitt Publishing Co., 130 pp. (Excellent)

Mitchell, Roger, 1983 Grand Canyon Jeep Trails I. Glendale, CA: La Siesta Press, 47 pp. [This slim volume covers most of the major jeep trails on the North Rim of the Canyon, particularly in the area of the Shivwits Plateau. I only wish someone would put together a more comprehensive guide...]

Ohlman, J. R., (nd) [a collection of Jim's Grand Canyon hiking and climbing logs, correspondence and history files]

Peattie, Roderick (ed.), 1984 The Inverted Mountains: Canyons of the West. New York, NY: Vanguard Press. [Several chapters on Grand

Canyon trails and their history]

Powell, J. W., 1961 The Exploration of the Colorado river and its Canyons. New York, NY: Dover Publications, Inc., 400 pp. (first published in 1895) [The classic river tale of those who first "ran the Grand Canyon" and for the most part lived to tell about it]

Purvis, L. L., 1989 The Ace in the Hole. Columbus, GA: Brentwood Christian Press, 142 pp. [All about the CCC occupation of the Canyon during the 1930's, with emphasis on construction of the River Trail, and Phantom Ranch area]

Rainbow Expeditions, 1980 Lee's Ferry, Arizona; a recreational map to a portion of the Grand Canyon National Park and vicinity. Tucson, AZ: Rainbow Expeditions, 2nd ed., (Map No. 1, Grand Canyon Recreational Map Series), 1 sheet. [A handy little map, especially in these days of 7.5' topographic quadrangles]

----------, 1980 Phantom Ranch, Arizona, a recreational map to a portion of the Grand Canyon National Park and vicinity. Tucson, AZ: Rainbow Expeditions, 2nd ed., (Map No. 4, Grand Canyon Recreational Map Series), 1 sheet. [Not nearly as useful as the Lee's Ferry map, but makes a great wall hanging]

Rusho, W. L., and Crampton, C. Gregory, 1975 Desert River Crossing: Historic Lee's Ferry on the Colorado River. Salt Lake City, UT: Peregrine Smith, Inc. [As with Measeles' book mentioned earlier, excellent. The two books should be consulted together for a more complete story]

Schwartz, D. W., Chapman, R. C., and Kepp, Jane, 1980 Archeology of the Grand Canyon: Unkar Delta. Santa Fe, NM: School of American Research Press. [There are dozens of important works on Grand Canyon prehistory, but this is the only one referenced in this guide. Consult Hughes (1978) and Spamer (1990) for a more complete listing]

Simmons, G. C., and Gaskill, D. L., 1972 River runners' guide to the canyons of the Green and Colorado Rivers, with emphasis on geologic features. V. 3, Marble Gorge and Grand Canyon. Denver, CO: Powell Society, 132 pp.

Smith, Dwight L., and Crampton, C. G., (eds.) 1987 The Colorado River Survey: Robert B. Stanton and the Denver, Colorado Canyon and

Pacific Railroad. Salt Lake City, UT: Howe Brothers, 305 pp. [An authoritative work on Stanton's 1889-90 river surveys. Refer also the reference section of Lavender's book for other sources of information on Stanton]

Southwest Natural and Cultural Heritage Association, (nd) Recreation Opportunity Guide - North Kaibab Ranger District: Kaibab National Forest, 114 pp. [An interesting little guide which may be picked up at the District Forest Office in Fredonia, or at the seasonal contact station at Jacob Lake]

Spamer, Earle, 1990 Bibliography of the Grand Canyon and the Lower Colorado River. Grand Canyon Natural History Association Monograph 8 (with supplements for 1992 and 1993). [Without a doubt, the most authoritative and exhaustive reference list for the Grand Canyon in existence. Anyone who has more than a passing interest in the Canyon, whether it be concerning the geology, biology, history, prehistory, or whatever will want to examine this work. A labor of love, truly worthy of the thousands of hours that went into its creation and maintenance]

Spangler, Sharon, 1986 On Foot in the Grand Canyon. Denver, CO: Pruitt Publishing. [Highly recommended reading for novice Grand Canyon hikers and for those who would like to bone up on their history. Written by an average hiker for the average hiker]

Steck, George, 1989 Grand Canyon Loop Hikes I. Evergreen, CO: Chockstone Press, 108 pp. [An excellent guide which covers the area between Bright Angel and Kanab Creeks]

Steck, George, 1993 Grand Canyon Loop Hikes II. Evergreen, CO: Chockstone Press, 262 pp. [Covers select trips form North Bass to Tuckup and from Rider Canyon to Eminence Break. Also includes a mega hike from Nankoweap to Bright Angel]

Stevens, Larry, 1983 The Colorado River in Grand Canyon; a comprehensive guide to its natural and human history. Flagstaff, AZ: Red Lake Books; 2nd ed., 1984, 107 pp.; 3rd ed., 1987, 110 pp. [Currently, the best all around river guide available]

Suran, Bill, 1991 The Kolb Brothers of Grand Canyon. Grand Canyon Natural History Association, 60 pp. [A short, anecdotal history of the Kolbs photographic business and their jaunts into the Canyon]

Sutphen, Debra, 1991a "Grandview, Hermit and South Kaibab Trails:

linking the past, present, and future at the Grand Canyon of the Colorado, 1880-1990." Flagstaff, AZ: M. S. thesis, unpublished, Northern Arizona University, 164 pp.

----------, 1991b "Too Hard a Nut to Crack; Peter D. Berry and the Battle for Free Enterprise at the Grand Canyon." *Journal of Arizona History II,* V. 32, no. 2, pp. 153-172.

----------, 1992a "Kaibab Suspension Bridge," unpub. manuscript (Summer, 1992) [This paper, along with the two which follow are available at the NPS Library, Grand Canyon]

----------, 1992b "North Kaibab Trail," unpub. manuscript (Summer, 1992)

----------, 1992c "Red Canyon/New Hance Trail," unpub. manuscript (Summer, 1992)

Thayer, David, 1986 A Guide to Grand Canyon Geology along Bright Angel Trail. Grand Canyon Natural History Association, 66 pp.

Thybony, Scott, 1985 A Guide to Inner Canyon Hiking. Grand Canyon Natural History Association (3rd ed.) [The original and most compact guide to the trails of the Central Grand Canyon]

Trimble, Marshall, 1986 Roadside History of Arizona. Missoula, MT: Mountain Press Publishing Co., 480 pp. [Compact, but not entirely accurate or exhaustive]

U. S. Geological Survey, 1926 Plan and Profile Map of the Little Colorado River from Tolchico Dam to the Confluence [This map is very difficult to find, but it gives the earliest depiction of the trails and routes of the Little Colorado Gorge I know of]

Verkamp, Margaret, 1943 The History of Grand Canyon National Park. Tucson, AZ: University of Arizona, unpub. manuscript thesis, 70 pp. [Republished by Grand Canyon Pioneers Society, 1993] {Prior to Hughes' work on Grand Canyon history, this was the reference of choice, and still makes a good one to read}

Wampler, Joseph, 1959 Havasu Canyon: Gem of the Grand Canyon. Berkeley, CA: Howell-North Press, 121 pp. [A little known guidebook which outline several out of the way trips in Havasu Canyon. The Havasupai used to sell this book at their village store, but that may no longer be true]

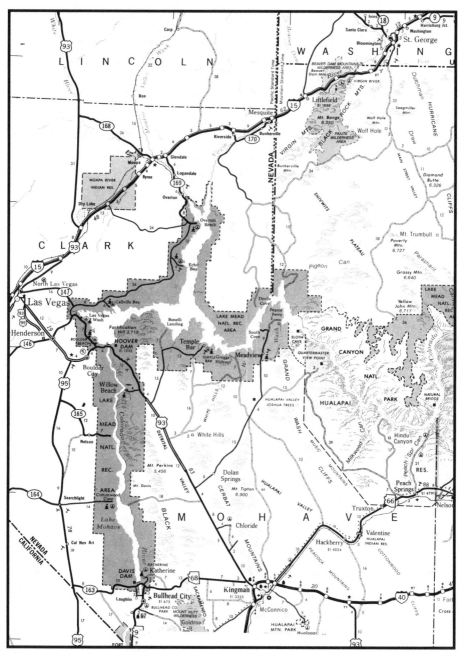

Road map of northwestern Arizona
Map courtesy of Arizona Highways

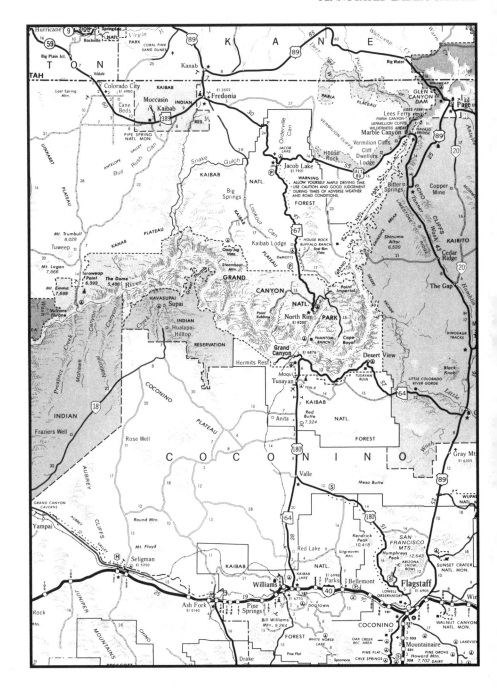

185

Flood damage of August 4 – 5, 1948. Washout on Bright Angel Trail about 2 miles down from South Rim. Foreman H.B. Chase shown.

Photo By: J.M. Eden, NPS, Aug. 9, 1948

Grand Canyon National Park #1562

Index

189

Overhanging cliff; Kanab Creek. Kanab is one of the longer tributaries to Grand Canyon, but is dry for the most part below Fredonia, Arizona.

191

Line shack near the Cane Spring Trail.

193

Red Pockets Mountain south of Mesquite, Nevada. Photo taken near Brumley Well.

Hikers wishing correspondence with the author or editor should write:

J.D. Green

c/o Tower of Ra Publishing

1501 Tina Lane

Kissimmee, Florida 34744-5026

Jim Ohlman

P.O. Box 1451

Kayenta, Arizona 86033

Cougar Spring Trail below Mount Bangs (Hancock Peak).

A view of Grand Canyon from Price Point.
Photo By: G. Henshaw

Mile 136.
Photo By: G. Henshaw

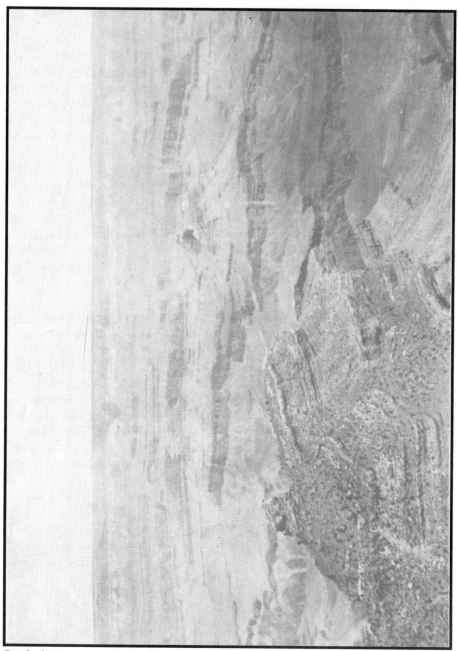

Battleship.
Photo By: G. Langdale, 1944